Teacher's guide to Book 9S

Contents

CAMBRIDGE
UNIVERSITY PRESS

PUBLISHED BY THE PRESS SYNDICATE OF THE UNIVERSITY OF CAMBRIDGE
The Pitt Building, Trumpington Street, Cambridge, United Kingdom

CAMBRIDGE UNIVERSITY PRESS
The Edinburgh Building, Cambridge CB2 2RU, UK
40 West 20th Street, New York, NY 10011–4211, USA
477 Williamstown Road, Port Melbourne, VIC 3207, Australia
Ruiz de Alarcón 13, 28014 Madrid, Spain
Dock House, The Waterfront, Cape Town 8001, South Africa

http://www.cambridge.org

First published 2003
Reprinted 2003

Printed in the United Kingdom at the University Press, Cambridge

Typeface Minion   *System* QuarkXPress®

A catalogue record for this book is available from the British Library

ISBN 0 521 53816 5 paperback

Typesetting and technical illustrations by The School Mathematics Project
Photograph on page 10 by Graham Portlock
Cover image © ImageState Ltd
Cover design by Angela Ashton

The following people contributed to the writing of the SMP Interact key stage 3 materials.

Ben Alldred	Ian Edney	John Ling	Susan Shilton
Juliette Baldwin	Steve Feller	Carole Martin	Caroline Starkey
Simon Baxter	Rose Flower	Peter Moody	Liz Stewart
Gill Beeney	John Gardiner	Lorna Mulhern	Pam Turner
Roger Beeney	Bob Hartman	Mary Pardoe	Biff Vernon
Roger Bentote	Spencer Instone	Peter Ransom	Jo Waddingham
Sue Briggs	Liz Jackson	Paul Scruton	Nigel Webb
David Cassell	Pamela Leon	Richard Sharpe	Heather West

Others, too numerous to mention individually, gave valuable advice, particularly by commenting on and trialling draft materials.

Editorial team	**Project administrator**	**Design**	**Project support**
David Cassell	Ann White	Pamela Alford	Carol Cole
Spencer Instone		Melanie Bull	Pam Keetch
John Ling		Nicky Lake	Jane Seaton
Paul Scruton		Tiffany Passmore	Cathy Syred
Susan Shilton		Martin Smith	
Caroline Starkey			
Heather West			

Special thanks go to Colin Goldsmith.

Introduction

Teaching approaches

SMP Interact sets out to help teachers use a variety of teaching approaches in order to stimulate pupils and foster their understanding and enjoyment of mathematics.

A central place is given to discussion and other interactive work. In this respect and others the material supports the methodology of the *Framework for teaching mathematics*. Questions that promote effective discussion and activities well suited to group work occur throughout the material.

Some activities, mostly where a new idea or technique is introduced, are described only in the teacher's guide. (These are indicated in the pupils' book by a solid marginal strip – see below.)

Materials

There are three series in key stage 3: books 7T–9T cover up to national curriculum level 5; 7S–9S go up to level 6; 7C–9C go up to level 7, though schools have successfully prepared pupils for level 8 with them, drawing lightly on extra topics from early in the *SMP Interact* GCSE course.

Pupils' books

Each unit of work begins with a statement of learning objectives and most units end with questions for self assessment.

 Teacher-led activities that are described in the teacher's guide are denoted by a solid marginal strip in both the pupil's book and the teacher's guide.

 Some other activities that are expected to need teacher support are marked by a broken strip.

Where the writers have particular classroom organisation in mind (for example working in pairs or groups), this is stated in the pupils' book.

Resource sheets

Resource sheets, some essential and some optional, are linked to some activities in the books.

Practice booklets

For each book there is a practice booklet containing further questions unit by unit. These booklets are particularly suitable for homework.

Teacher's guides

For each unit, there is usually an overview, details of any essential or optional equipment, including resource sheets, and the practice book page references, followed by guidance that includes detailed descriptions of teacher-led activities, advice on difficult ideas and comments from teachers who trialled the material.

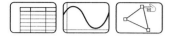

There is scope to use computers and graphic calculators throughout the material. These symbols mark specific opportunities to use a spreadsheet, graph plotter and dynamic geometry software respectively.

Answers to questions in the pupil's book and the practice booklet follow. For reasons of economy answers to resource sheets that pupils write on are not always given in the teacher's guide; they can of course be written on a spare copy of the sheet.

Assessment

Unit by unit assessment tests are available both as hard copy and and as editable files on CD (details are at www.smpmaths.org.uk). The practice booklets are also suitable as an assessment resource.

Oral and mental starters

An oral or mental starter can be used for a number of purposes.

- It can **introduce the main topic**, and many of the teacher-led activities described in this guide can be used in this way.
- It can also be an effective way of **revising skills that are needed for the main topic** and can prevent the subsequent lesson 'sagging' when those skills falter. For example, a 'spider diagram' can be used as shown on the next page to revise substitution before work on changing the subject of a simple formula (Unit 5) or on trial and improvement (Unit 23).
- Alternatively a starter can be used to **revise skills that are unrelated to the main lesson**. Some questions and activities in the pupil's book can be adapted for later use as starters. For example, question F5 on page 71 can be used with other sets of four equations.

Starter formats

The formats described below have been found very effective and can be adapted to different topics.

Small whiteboards ('show me boards') and markers are invaluable for many types of starter, for example *True or false?*, *What am I?* and *Odd one out*. Pupils write their responses on their board and hold it up, giving you instant feedback on the whole class.

True or false?

You say or write a statement (such as 'A cube has three planes of symmetry.' or '$5(n + 7) = 5n + 7$') and pupils decide if it is true or false.

Spider diagram

You write a whole number, fraction, decimal, percentage, word, algebraic expression … in a circle on the board. This is the spider's body. The ends of the legs can be completed in a variety of ways.

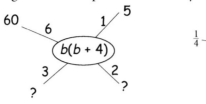

Today's number is …

Write a number on the board and put a ring round it. It could be a whole number, decimal or fraction. Pupils make up calculations with that number as the result. Calculations can be restricted to a particular type. A variation of this format is *Today's expression is …*

What am I?

For example, 'I am a three digit number. I am a power of 2. The sum of my digits is 13. What am I?'

Ordering

Pupils put a set of numbers such as $\frac{1}{10}$, 0.6, $\frac{1}{2}$, 0.32 in order of size.

Matching

Pupils match up a set (such as this one) into pairs or larger groups.

| $a(a + 4)$ | $4(a + 2)$ | $a(a + 8)$ | $a^2 + 8a$ | $a^2 + 4a$ | $4a + 8$ |

Target number

Pupils are given a set of numbers or choose them themselves.
A 'target' number is chosen. Pupils try to make the target number using the given numbers and any of the four operations. (Not all numbers need be used but each may be used only once.)
For example, make 542 from these.

2   7   8   4   1   100

Bingo

Pupils choose numbers from a given set and fill in their bingo 'card' with them. The card can hold as many numbers as you choose.

In this example, fractions have been chosen from a given set of fifteen. You could 'call':

- $\frac{1}{2}$ of $1\frac{1}{2}$
- The fraction half way between $\frac{1}{3}$ and $\frac{2}{3}$

$\frac{1}{2}$		$\frac{1}{3}$
	$\frac{1}{6}$	
$\frac{2}{5}$		$\frac{3}{4}$

Counting stick

A counting stick is marked in equal intervals, usually in two contrasting colours. You can show pupils a starting point, tell them the value of one interval and then ask them to identify numbers you point to. For example, you could tell them one interval on this stick is 0.05 .

?   ?   ?   ?   1.1   ?   ?

Alternatively, give the values of two key points (Blu-tack labels on) and indicate points at random, each time asking for the value.

Array

This is a set of numbers, fractions, expressions … arranged in a grid or just in a list, on which you base questions, for example:

- Find two expressions that multiply to give $5n + 15$.
- Add up the expressions in the middle row.
- Which three expressions in a row add to give $4n + 5$?

$n+5$	$5n$	5
$n-7$	n	$n-2$
2	$n+3$	$3n$

Odd one out

Pupils identify the odd one out from a set, such as 25, 36, 49, 20, 16 .

Two-way property table

The headings of a two-way table like this one are shown on the board and pupils say what should go in the cells. It is often best to say that all the entries should be different.

	A multiple of 2	A power of 3
A factor of 18		
A square number		

Topics for starters

Below, arranged by some broad topic areas, are suggestions for other ways the starter formats can be used.

Number relationships

Bingo Use 'calls' like:

- the cube of 4
- the square root of 81
- the cube root of 8

Odd one out Present sets such as 11, 13, 15, 17, 23, 29 and 4, 8, 64, 28, 32 .

Algebraic manipulation

True or false? For example, $8n + 2 = 10n$ (which may, of course, produce the response 'Sometimes')

Today's expression is … Pupils have to find combinations of expressions that are equivalent to a given expression. For example 'Today's expression is $6n$' could lead to $8n - 2n$, $2 \times 3n$, $12n \div 2$ and so on.

Matching A set of expressions or formulas has to be sorted into groups or pairs of equivalent expressions or formulas.

Fractions

True or false? For example, $\frac{1}{2} + \frac{1}{3} = \frac{2}{5}$

Today's number is … Pupils have to devise calculations that result in a given fraction.

Ordering The set can consist entirely of fractions.

Matching A set of fractions (or fraction calculations) is to be sorted into equivalent groups or pairs.

Counting stick The stick can be marked off in fractions.

Percentages

Spider diagram A percentage can be put on the body and that percentage of various amounts at the ends of the legs.

Matching A set of increases, decreases and multipliers can be sorted into equivalent pairs.

True or false? For example, $\frac{1}{3} = 33\%$

Ordering For example, 0.65, $\frac{1}{4}$, 20%, $\frac{1}{3}$, 40%

Bingo Questions called are 'What is 20% of 30?', 'Increase 40 by 50%' and so on.

Decimals and measures

Array Use a set of decimals.

Today's number is … Pupils have to devise calculations that result in a given decimal.

True or false? For example, $0.9 \times 7 = 0.63$, $0.2 \times 0.3 = 0.6$

Odd one out Use a set of measures such as 1.3 m, 1.30 m, 1.03 m, 130 cm.

Spatial visualisation

What am I? I have a hexagonal cross-section for most of my length and you probably carry one of me around with you; what am I?
I am a solid with six rectangular faces; what am I?
I have one square face and four triangular faces; what am I?
I have eight triangular faces; what am I?

1 Solids

Essential	**Optional**
A selection of objects similar to those shown in the pupil's book	Water in a suitable container (a three-litre plastic fizzy drinks bottle, cut off below its 'shoulders', works well) Potatoes, carrots or similar and a sharp knife Plasticine
Practice booklet pages 3 to 5	

A Cross-sections (p 4)

◊ Use the photos and drawings of the screwdriver to discuss what a cross-section is. Emphasise the idea of cutting through the object at the water level. Many teachers have found cutting through vegetables an effective approach at this stage. Shapes causing difficulty can be reproduced as Plasticine models that are then sliced through.

Some pupils may need guidance about how accurate their sketches need to be. Explain that exact drawings are not required, but try to get over the idea that each sequence of sketches should show the relative sizes of the cross-sections of a particular object.

A4 After doing this pupils can draw a set of cross-sections of an object of their own choice.

A5 The set of cross-sections labelled A can lead to a more general discussion of solids which, when lowered into the water a certain way round, produce a cross-section that doesn't change. Can pupils think of some?

A8 Pupils find the chair difficult, partly because they are not expecting anything quite so big. You may need to give a hint or gesture that 'it's about this big'.

'To start the lesson I asked for a volunteer… I then brought out my saw and pretended to "cut in half" at knee level and asked [the] class to draw the cross-section… The next cut was at elbow level… the next cut across the shoulders. The final cut was through the head. There was no shortage of volunteers.'

B Prisms (p 9)

◊ Defining 'prism' is harder than defining 'cuboid'. This is a task which could be set to pupils working in pairs or groups. It is useful to have a number of three-dimensional shapes available to help clarify later what is and what is not a prism. Have some counter-examples ready; for example, the suggested definition 'same shape all through' can be met with a twisted pile of paper.

◊ The only prisms used at this stage are 'right' prisms, where a plane shape (the cross-section) is translated in a direction perpendicular to its plane.

B5 It emerges that $1\,cm^3 = 1000\,mm^3$. You can ask the class to consider why.

C Planes of symmetry (p 11)

◊ There are various ways of giving a practical demonstration. You can place a solid made from multilink against a mirror and observe that the 'object' consisting of the solid and its reflection has a plane of symmetry – the mirror. Alternatively, you can use objects that can be cut (for example, Plasticine models).

A Cross-sections (p 4)

A1 C, A, B then D

A2 B, C, D then A

A3 Trowel   Hoe   Mallet

A4 C, A, D, B then E

A5 1 B, 2 C, 3 A

A6 (a)   (b)

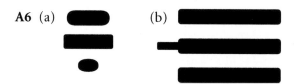

A7 1 A, 2 B, 3 A, 4 C, 5 A, 6 B

A8 (a) (i) Fork   (ii) Chair

B Prisms (p 9)

B1 (a) $60\,cm^3$ (b) $98\,cm^3$ (c) $125\,cm^3$
(d) $40\,cm^3$ (e) $96\,cm^3$

B2 (a) $48\,cm^3$ (b) $84\,cm^3$

B3 The pupil's sketches, leading to these surface areas
(a) $124\,cm^2$ (b) $136\,cm^2$

B4 (a) $60\,\text{cm}^3$ (b) $94.5\,\text{cm}^3$ (c) $180\,\text{cm}^3$
(d) $60\,\text{cm}^3$

B5 (a) $60\,000\,\text{mm}^3$ (b) $94\,500\,\text{mm}^3$
(c) $180\,000\,\text{mm}^3$ (d) $60\,000\,\text{mm}^3$
The numbers have been multiplied by 1000.

ℂ **Planes of symmetry** (p 11)

C1 4

C2 4

C3 3

What progress have you made? (p 12)

1 E, C, A, B, F, D or B, E, C, A, F, D

2 (a)

(b)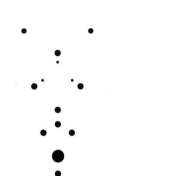

3 Volume $= 32\,\text{cm}^3$, surface area $= 72\,\text{cm}^2$

4 5

Practice booklet

Section A (p 3)

1 Set 1: slotted spoon D, C, A, B, E
Set 2: spatula A, D, E, C, B
 (A, D and E could be in any order.)
Set 3: fish slice C, D, A, E, B

2

3 (a) (b) All will be like this.

4 Some possible drawings:

Pencil 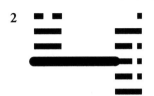 Safety pin

Padlock

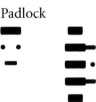

5 A sphere

Section B (p 5)

1 (a) $46\,\text{cm}^3$ (b) $36\,\text{cm}^3$ (c) $90\,\text{cm}^3$

2 (a) (i) $30\,\text{cm}^3$ (ii) $74\,\text{cm}^2$
(b) (i) $42\,\text{cm}^3$ (ii) $110\,\text{cm}^2$

Section C (p 5)

1 (a) 1 (b) 4

Equivalent expressions

Practice booklet pages 6 to 9

Ⓐ **Multiplying out brackets 1** (p 13)

◊ The set of expressions $2n + 1$, $2n + 2$, $2n + 4$, $2(n + 1)$, $2(n + 2)$ and $2(n + 4)$ can be investigated using a spreadsheet as shown on page 2 (or just by filling in a table). Pupils choose values for n and compare the values of each expression. They will find that, say, $2n + 2 = 2(n + 1)$ for each value of n, and can review multiplying out brackets.

Other sets of expressions can be tried, for example: $3n - 1$, $3n - 3$, $3n - 9$, $3(n - 1)$, $3(n - 3)$ and $3(n - 9)$.

You can make the point that a statement like $2(3n + 2) = 6n + 4$ is an example of an identity: it is true for all values of n (unlike a statement like $3n + 2 = 11$, which we refer to as an equation and which is only true for one value of n).

Ⓑ **Multiplying out brackets 2** (p 15)

◊ The diagrams can be used to illustrate the expansions of $n(n + 2)$ and $p(p - 1)$: the area of the whole garden is $n(n + 2)$ or $n^2 + 2n$ (adding the area of the lawn and flower bed) and the area of the pool is $p(p - 1)$ or $p^2 - p$ (subtracting the paved area from the whole area).

Ⓒ **Factorising** (p 16)

D Fractions (p 17)

◊ A table (or spreadsheet) can be used to investigate the equivalence of the expressions at the top of the columns. A diagram like this can be useful.

$6n \rightarrow$ [bags] $\div 2 \rightarrow$ [bags] $\rightarrow 3n$ So $\dfrac{6n}{2} = 3n$

E Adding and subtracting fractions (p 18)

F True to form (p 19)

Pupils use the algebraic manipulation developed in earlier sections to prove statements about multiples, odd, even and prime numbers.

◊ Pupils could work in groups and report their findings on statements A to M to the class. They should try and justify their decisions. At the end of the discussion, pupils should be able to use simple algebraic arguments to classify the statements on the page as *always*, *sometimes* or *never* true.

• Always true: A, B, F, G, J

• Sometimes true and sometimes false: D, H, I

• Never true: C, E, K, L, M

A Multiplying out brackets 1 (p 13)

A1 $4(n + 3)$ and $4n + 12$

A2 (a) $2n + 10$ (b) $3n - 12$ (c) $6n + 12$
(d) $5n - 15$ (e) $4n + 4$ (f) $30 + 10n$
(g) $14 - 2n$ (h) $9 - 3n$

A3 $5p - 5$ and $5(p - 1)$

A4 (a) $6n$ (b) $15n$ (c) $16n$ (d) $30n$

A5 (a) $6n + 4$ (b) $12n - 15$
(c) $10n + 5$ (d) $12n - 20$

A6 (a) $3n + 1$ (b) $2n + 3$ (c) $6n + 5$

A7 (a) 6
(b) A completed table with 2, 8, 10, 20 in the second column
(c) 'The output is twice the input' or output = 2 × input
(d) (i) The pupil's completed arrow diagram with the output $2(n + 5) - 10$ simplified to $2n$

(ii) The pupil's explanation such as, 'An input of n will always produce an output of $2n$ which is double the input.'

A8 (a) 20
(b) (i) $4(n - 1) + 4$ simplified to $4n$
(ii) 'The output is four times the input' or output = 4 × input. This rule will always work as an input of n always produces an output of $4n$.

A9 (a) 12
(b) A completed table with 6, 18, 60 in the second column
(c) 'The output is six times the input' or output = 6 × input
(d) (i) The pupil's completed arrow diagram with the output $2(3n + 4) - 8$ simplified to $6n$

(ii) The pupil's explanation such as, 'An input of n will always produce an output of $6n$ which is six times the input.'

B Multiplying out brackets 2 (p 15)

B1 (a) $x(x + 3)$ (b) $x^2 + 3x$

     (c) $x(x - 3)$ (d) $x^2 - 3x$

B2 $n^2 + 5n$

B3 $k^2 - 7k$

B4 (a) $n^2 + 4n$ (b) $m^2 + 7m$ (c) $x^2 - 6x$

     (d) $h^2 - 4h$ (e) $3b + b^2$ (f) $y + y^2$

     (g) $5a - a^2$ (h) $k - k^2$

B5 (a) (i) $2n,\ n + 6$ (ii) $3,\ n + 2$

     (b) (i) $k^2,\ 3k$ (ii) $k,\ k + 3$

     (c) (i) $2m - 4,\ 4m - 5$ (ii) $3,\ 2m - 3$

     (d) (i) $h^2 + 4h,\ h$ (ii) $h,\ h + 5$

*B6 (a) $5n + 15$ (b) $n^2 + 5n$

C Factorising (p 16)

C1 (a) $3a + 6 = 3(a + \mathbf{2})$

     (b) $5a - 15 = 5(a - \mathbf{3})$

     (c) $4a + 20 = \mathbf{4}(a + 5)$

C2 (a) $2(n + 7)$ (b) $5(n - 4)$

     (c) $3(n + 7)$ (d) $4(n - 1)$

C3 (a) $3(n + 6)$ (b) $n + 6$

C4 (a) $6a + 9 = 3(2a + \mathbf{3})$

     (b) $10a - 5 = \mathbf{5}(2a - 1)$

     (c) $8a + 20 = 4(\mathbf{2a} + 5)$

C5 (a) $2(2n + 5)$ (b) $3(3n - 2)$

     (c) $2(5n - 1)$ (d) $5(3n + 5)$

C6 (a) $4(2h + 3)$ (b) $2h + 3$

C7 (a) $a^2 + 6a = a(a + \mathbf{6})$

     (b) $k^2 - 3k = k(\mathbf{k} - 3)$

     (c) $n^2 + 5n = n(\mathbf{n} + \mathbf{5})$

C8 (a) $n(n + 3)$ (b) $b(b - 2)$

     (c) $a(a + 1)$ (d) $x(8 + x)$

C9 (a) $4(3n + 2)$ (b) $7(n - 1)$

     (c) $n(n + 8)$ (d) $n(n - 1)$

D Fractions (p 17)

D1 $\dfrac{9x}{3},\ \dfrac{12x}{4},\ \dfrac{15x}{5}$

D2 (a) $5n$ (b) $2n$ (c) $5n$ (d) $2n$ (e) $6n$

D3 (a) $\dfrac{n}{3} = \dfrac{2n}{\mathbf{6}}$ (b) $\dfrac{n}{5} = \dfrac{\mathbf{3n}}{15}$

     (c) $\dfrac{n}{4} = \dfrac{\mathbf{3n}}{12}$ (d) $\dfrac{n}{7} = \dfrac{\mathbf{5n}}{35}$

D4 $\dfrac{2a}{8},\ \dfrac{4a}{16},\ \dfrac{3a}{12}$

D5 (a) $\dfrac{n}{5} = \dfrac{2n}{\mathbf{10}}$ (b) $\dfrac{n}{3} = \dfrac{\mathbf{3n}}{9}$

     (c) $\dfrac{n}{2} = \dfrac{7n}{\mathbf{14}}$ (d) $\dfrac{n}{4} = \dfrac{\mathbf{5n}}{20}$

E Adding and subtracting fractions (p 18)

E1 (a) $\dfrac{3}{5}$ (b) $\dfrac{a + 1}{5}$

     (c) $\dfrac{3 - b}{5}$ (d) $\dfrac{a + b}{5}$

E2 (a) $\dfrac{a}{2} - \dfrac{1}{4} = \dfrac{\mathbf{2a}}{4} - \dfrac{1}{4} = \dfrac{\mathbf{2a - 1}}{4}$

     (b) $\dfrac{2}{9} + \dfrac{x}{3} = \dfrac{2}{9} + \dfrac{\mathbf{3x}}{9} = \dfrac{\mathbf{2 + 3x}}{9}$

E3 $\dfrac{2 + k}{8}$

E4 (a) $\dfrac{4a + 1}{8}$ (b) $\dfrac{1 + 3b}{6}$

     (c) $\dfrac{n + 2}{10}$ (d) $\dfrac{2a - b}{4}$

What progress have you made? (p 19)

1 (a) $2n + 10$ (b) $3n - 6$

     (c) $20n + 12$ (d) $5 - 10n$

     (e) $n^2 + 7n$ (f) $n^2 - 3n$

2 (a) $2(x + 7)$ (b) $3(x - 3)$

     (c) $2(3x + 2)$ (d) $5(2x - 3)$

     (e) $x(x + 8)$ (f) $x(x - 6)$

3 (a) $4n$ (b) $3p$ (c) $4t$

4 (a) $\dfrac{3 + m}{4}$ (b) $\dfrac{n - 1}{6}$

     (c) $\dfrac{2 + a}{4}$ (d) $\dfrac{2b - 1}{10}$

Practice booklet

Sections A and B (p 6)

1 $6(x + 5)$ and $6x + 30$

2 (a) $3n + 6$ (b) $5n - 15$ (c) $6n - 6$
   (d) $14 + 2n$ (e) $10n + 6$ (f) $9 + 12n$
   (g) $8n - 20$ (h) $10n + 2$

3 $3x - 6$ and $3(x - 2)$

4 (a) 12
   (b) A completed table with 9, 15, 30 in the second column
   (c) 'The output is three times the input' or output = 3 × input
   (d) (i) The pupil's completed arrow diagram with the output $3(n - 2) + 6$ simplified to $3n$
       (ii) The pupil's explanation such as, 'An input of n will always produce an output of $3n$ which is three times the input.'

5 (a) 24
   (b) A completed table with 8, 16, 80 in the second column
   (c) 'The output is eight times the input' or output = 8 × input
   (d) (i) The pupil's completed arrow diagram with the output $4(2n + 3) - 12$ simplified to $8n$
       (ii) The pupil's explanation such as, 'An input of n will always produce an output of $8n$ which is eight times the input.'

6 (a) $n^2 + 5n$ (b) $m^2 - 3m$
   (c) $k^2\ k$ (d) $4h + h^2$

7 (a) (i) $3n + 6, n + 2$ (ii) $4, n + 2$
   (b) (i) $x^2 - 5x, 2x$ (ii) $x, x - 3$

8 (a) $n^2 + 4n$ (b) $2x + 10$ (c) $9y - 15$
   (d) $a^2 - 6a$ (e) $6b + b^2$ (f) $10m + 5$
   (g) $3p - p^2$ (h) $6 - 6q$

Section C (p 8)

1 $2n + 8 = 2(n + \mathbf{4})$

2 (a) $2(n + 5)$ (b) $4(m - 3)$
   (c) $5(4 + x)$ (d) $6(y - 1)$

3 $6a + 15 = 3(\mathbf{2a} + 5)$

4 (a) $2(3p + 5)$ (b) $5(2a - 3)$
   (c) $2(4b + 1)$ (d) $4(3q - 2)$

5 (a) $5(2p + 5)$ (b) $2p + 5$

6 $h^2 + 6h = h(\mathbf{h + 6})$

7 (a) $x(x + 7)$ (b) $y(y - 5)$
   (c) $p(p + 1)$ (d) $q(2 + q)$

8 (a) $3(n + 7)$ (b) $5(3m - 2)$
   (c) $h(h + 4)$ (d) $9(1 + 2k)$
   (e) $w(w - 6)$ (f) $p(p - 1)$
   (g) $3(2n - 1)$ (h) $n(6 + n)$

Sections D and E (p 8)

1 (a) $4p$ (b) $4q$ (c) $5a$ (d) $5b$

2 $\dfrac{2x}{6}, \dfrac{4x}{12}, \dfrac{3x}{9}$

3 (a) $\dfrac{k}{4} = \dfrac{\mathbf{3k}}{\mathbf{12}}$ (b) $\dfrac{n}{2} = \dfrac{\mathbf{5n}}{10}$
   (c) $\dfrac{m}{3} = \dfrac{\mathbf{4m}}{12}$

4 (a) $\dfrac{h + 3}{4}$ (b) $\dfrac{a - 5}{6}$ (c) $\dfrac{n + 2p}{5}$

5 (a) $\dfrac{2}{3} = \dfrac{\mathbf{4}}{6}$ (b) $\dfrac{n + 4}{6}$

6 (a) $\dfrac{b}{3} = \dfrac{\mathbf{2b}}{6}$ (b) $\dfrac{2b + 1}{6}$

7 (a) $\dfrac{x}{5} = \dfrac{\mathbf{2x}}{10}$ (b) $\dfrac{2x - y}{10}$

8 (a) $\dfrac{h + 4}{8}$ (b) $\dfrac{2a - 3}{10}$ (c) $\dfrac{3n + p}{12}$

Section F (p 9)

1 A and F are always true;
   B, D and E are sometimes true and sometimes false;
   C is never true.

③ Fractions

Essential

Sheet 254

Practice booklet pages 10 to 12

Ⓐ Calculating with fractions – a reminder (p 20)

Ⓑ Fraction of a fraction (p 21)

Sheet 254 (2 copies per pupil)

Although the routine process for multiplying fractions is easy to remember and carry out (multiply top numbers and multiply bottom numbers), many pupils lack a sense of what is happening with the fractions and this can lead to errors of magnitude in decimal multiplications going uncorrected. The square shading approach helps build the necessary understanding. It also makes it clear that fraction of a fraction (or multiplication of fractions) is a commutative operation.

However, pupils need to be using the routine process and no longer dependent on shaded squares before attempting questions that involve the inverse of multiplication (B17 and B19).

Ⓒ Flows (p 24)

This contains further fraction multiplication problems

Ⓓ Thinking backwards (p 25)

Several of these questions involve the inverse of multiplication by a fraction. All of them can be solved by the routine process for division by a fraction, taking for example, D1 to be $18 \div \frac{3}{4}$, then inverting and multiplying.
(The same is true of B17 and B19). However it is better to use inverse examples such as these to cultivate thinking skills: 'If 18 panes are $\frac{3}{4}$ then $\frac{1}{4}$ is 6 panes so the whole window is 24 panes.'

Ⓐ Calculating with fractions – a reminder (p 20)

A1 (a) $\frac{8}{15}$ (b) $\frac{7}{12}$ (c) $\frac{11}{15}$
  (d) $\frac{31}{40}$ (e) $\frac{14}{30}$ or $\frac{7}{15}$

A2 (a) $\frac{9}{20}$ (b) $\frac{11}{20}$

A3 (a) $\frac{19}{24}$ (b) $\frac{5}{24}$

A4 $14\frac{1}{4}''$

A5 (a) $\frac{7}{12}$ (b) $\frac{1}{12}$ (c) $\frac{5}{12}$

Egyptian fractions

These are some possibilities.
There are others.

$\frac{5}{8} = \frac{1}{2} + \frac{1}{8}$

$\frac{7}{8} = \frac{1}{2} + \frac{1}{4} + \frac{1}{8}$

$\frac{7}{12} = \frac{1}{2} + \frac{1}{12}$ or $\frac{1}{3} + \frac{1}{4}$

$\frac{17}{30} = \frac{1}{2} + \frac{1}{15}$ or $\frac{1}{3} + \frac{1}{6} + \frac{1}{15}$

$\frac{4}{5} = \frac{1}{2} + \frac{1}{5} + \frac{1}{10}$

Ⓑ Fraction of a fraction (p 21)

B1 $\frac{1}{6}$

B2 (a), (b)   (c) $\frac{1}{20}$

B3 (a) 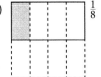 $\frac{1}{8}$ (b) 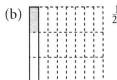 $\frac{1}{24}$

  (c) 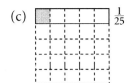 $\frac{1}{25}$

B4 (a)   (b)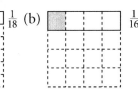

  (c) They both give the same result.

B5 (a) 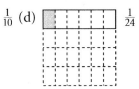 $\frac{1}{18}$ (b) $\frac{1}{16}$

  (c) $\frac{1}{10}$ (d) $\frac{1}{24}$

B6 (a) $\frac{1}{8}$ (b) $\frac{1}{3}$ (c) $\frac{1}{3}$ (d) $\frac{1}{6}$

B7 (a) $\frac{1}{4}$ (b) $\frac{1}{30}$ (c) $\frac{1}{32}$ (d) $\frac{1}{36}$

B8 (a) $\frac{1}{4} \times \frac{1}{3} = \frac{1}{12}$ (b) $\frac{1}{2} \times \frac{1}{4} = \frac{1}{8}$
  (c) $\frac{1}{6} \times \frac{1}{8} = \frac{1}{48}$

B9 (a) 40 (b) 10 (c) $\frac{1}{8}$
  (d) $\frac{1}{8}$ is $\frac{1}{4}$ of $\frac{1}{2}$ (or $\frac{1}{4} \times \frac{1}{2}$)

B10 $\frac{3}{20}$

B11 (a), (b)   (c) $\frac{3}{8}$

B12 Yes: $\frac{1}{3} \times \frac{5}{8}$ $\frac{5}{8} \times \frac{1}{3}$

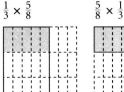

They both equal $\frac{5}{24}$.

B13 (a) 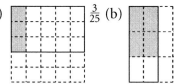 $\frac{3}{25}$ (b) $\frac{4}{15}$

(c) $\frac{8}{15}$

B14 (a) $\frac{3}{20}$ (b) 6

B15 Multiply the two numerators together to get the numerator for the answer. Multiply the denominators to get the denominator for the answer.

B16 (a) $\frac{4}{9}$ (b) $\frac{1}{2}$ (c) $\frac{2}{5}$ (d) $\frac{5}{9}$

B17 (a) $\frac{5}{6}$ (b) $\frac{3}{8}$ (c) $\frac{3}{4}$ (d) $\frac{7}{8}$

B18 (a) $\frac{5}{8}$ (b) $\frac{1}{16}$ (c) $\frac{1}{3}$ (d) $\frac{1}{5}$

*__B19__ (a) $\frac{3}{4}$ (b) $\frac{2}{3}$ (c) $\frac{4}{5}$ (d) $\frac{5}{6}$

Ⅽ **Flows** (p 24)

C1 (a) (i) $\frac{1}{4}$ (ii) $\frac{1}{4}$ (iii) $\frac{3}{8}$ (iv) $\frac{1}{8}$

(b) 1

(c) (i) 60 (ii) 60 (iii) 90 (iv) 30

C2 (a) $\frac{1}{15}$ (b) $\frac{2}{6}$ (or $\frac{1}{3}$) (c) $\frac{2}{6}$ (or $\frac{1}{3}$)

The pupil's check, showing that the four fractions add up to 1.

Ⅾ **Thinking backwards** (p 25)

D1 24

D2 10

D3 25

D4 (a) $\frac{5}{24}$ (b) 48

D5 10

D6 96

D7 84

*__D8__ (a) $\frac{1}{4}$ (b) $\frac{3}{4}$ (or $\frac{15}{20}$)

(c) $\frac{1}{3}$ (d) $\frac{2}{5}$

What progress have you made? (p 26)

1 (a) $\frac{3}{8}$ (b) $\frac{1}{3}$ (c) $\frac{1}{30}$

2 (a) $\frac{1}{30}$ (b) $\frac{3}{20}$ (c) $\frac{1}{4}$

3 $\frac{1}{3}$

4 (a) $\frac{2}{3}$ (b) $\frac{3}{4}$ (c) $\frac{1}{3}$

5 (a) $\frac{4}{15}$ (b) $\frac{1}{15}$ (c) $\frac{1}{2}$ (d) $\frac{1}{6}$

6 432 miles

Practice booklet

Sections B and C (p 10)

1 $\frac{1}{20}$

2 (a) $\frac{1}{12}$ (b) $\frac{1}{20}$ (c) $\frac{1}{30}$

3 (a) $\frac{1}{12}$ (b) $\frac{1}{40}$ (c) $\frac{1}{25}$

4 (a) $\frac{1}{3}$ (b) $\frac{1}{8}$ (c) $\frac{1}{6}$

5 (a) 20 (b) 5 (c) $\frac{1}{24}$

6 (a) $\frac{1}{3}$ or $\frac{2}{6}$ (b) 10

7 (a) $\frac{2}{15}$ (b) $\frac{9}{20}$ (c) $\frac{6}{40}$ or $\frac{3}{20}$

8 $\frac{3}{20}$

9 (a) $\frac{3}{10}$ (b) $\frac{1}{5}$ (c) $\frac{3}{10}$

(d) $\frac{3}{8}$ (e) $\frac{1}{2}$ (f) $\frac{3}{4}$

10 (a) $\frac{5}{12}$ (b) $\frac{2}{3}$ (c) $\frac{7}{10}$

11 (a) (i) $\frac{1}{40}$ (ii) $\frac{9}{40}$ (iii) $\frac{3}{5}$ (iv) $\frac{3}{20}$

(b) The pupil's check

Section D (p 11)

1 20

2 48

3 (a) $\frac{1}{6}$ (b) 48

4 45

5 (a) $\frac{1}{4}$ (b) $\frac{2}{3}$

6 (a) $\frac{2}{3}$ (b) $\frac{1}{3}$ (c) $\frac{2}{5}$ (d) $\frac{3}{4}$

As time goes by

Practice booklet pages 13 to 16

A Filling up (p 27)

◊ It is not intended that pupils think numerically about the narrower and wider jars. It would be difficult for them to understand at this stage that, say, the water level of a jar that is half as wide as the one on the page would rise four times as fast. It is enough for them to see that after 1 second the level would be higher than 2 cm so the line would be steeper for the narrower jar (and shallower for a wider jar).

B More filling (p 30)

The objective is for pupils to see that the water level begins to rise slowly but speeds up so that the graph is a curve that increases more and more quickly as time goes on.

◊ Pupils who find it hard to see that the graph must be a curve may find it helpful to think about the graph for the following approximation to the cone.

If the number of steps increases, the container approximates more closely to a cone and the graph of line segments approximates more closely to a curve.

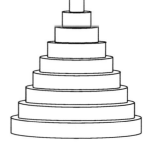

ℂ Diamonds are forever? (p 32)

𝔻 Speed graphs (p 33)

◊ You may wish to use the questions in D1 orally with the class as part of your introduction.

◊ When interpreting a speed–time graph, pupils frequently think that the shape of the graph reflects the terrain over which the cyclist, say, is travelling. So they expect that going slowly up a hill is shown by a 'hill' in the graph.

If this problem arises, you could try a 'point by point' approach. Suggest a 'story' such as 'Jay is cycling steadily, but then goes up a steep hill. She then cycles very quickly down the other side.' Sketch speed–time axes, and plot a first point for Jay's speed.

Point a little further along the time axes, ask 'She's cycling steadily. What is her speed compared with before?' and then plot the corresponding point. A little further along the time axis ask, 'She comes to a steep hill. What's her speed now compared with before?' and again plot the point.

Carry on like this until her whole journey has been discussed, and then join the points.

𝔸 Filling up (p 27)

A1 (a) 4.5 cm   (b) 7.5 cm

     (c) Straight-line graph through the points (0, 0) and (5, 7.5)

     (d) About 3.7 seconds

A2 (a) 3 cm   (b) 3 cm

     (c) Jar 1: 4 cm, Jar 2: 2 cm

     (d) Jar 1 is narrower with the pupil's explanation

A3 A, Q; B, P; C, R

A4 A

A5 A, Y; B, Z; C, X

A6 The pupil's sketch graph similar to

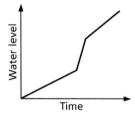

𝔹 More filling (p 30)

B1 A, R; B, Q; C, S; D, P

B2 A

B3 The pupil's sketch graphs similar to

(a)

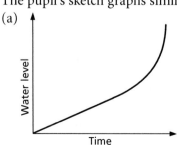

(b)

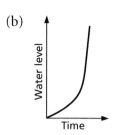

(c)

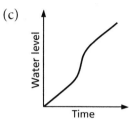

(d)

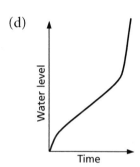

ℂ **Diamonds are forever?** (p 32)

C1 40 miles

C2 (a) (i) 90 miles
    (ii) The completed table with 50,
        90, 130, 170 in the last column

    (b) Straight-line graph for Sad Harry
        through the points (Midnight, 50)
        and (3 a.m., 170)

C3 (a) On the same axes, straight-line
        graph for Minnie through the points
        (Midnight, 0) and (3 a.m., 180)

    (b) 60 m.p.h.

C4 (a) 70 miles   (b) 30 miles
    (c) 40 miles   (d) 2.30 a.m.

C5 Sad Harry

𝔻 **Speed graphs** (p 33)

D1 (a) Hill View Road
    (b) School Road
    (c) (i) Clark Road
        (ii) 2 minutes

D2 (a) 50 minutes
    (b) 30 and 40 minutes
    (c) 60 and 70 minutes

D3

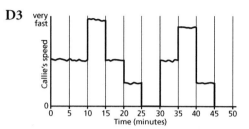

D4 (a) Graph B
    (b) The pupil's stories for A and C

D5

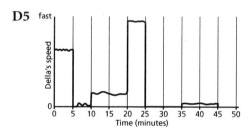

What progress have you made? (p 36)

1 (a) A, P; B, Q; C, R
   (b)

2

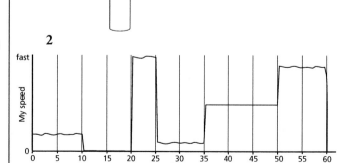

Practice booklet

Sections A and B (p 13)

    1 A, Q; B, R; C, P

    2 A, Graph 2; B, Graph 1; C, Graph 3

    3 (a)   (b)

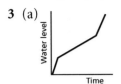 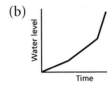

    4 Graph 2

    5 The pupil's sketch graph similar to

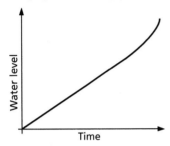

Section C (p 15)

    1 30 miles

    2 Car A: 30 miles; Car B: 40 miles;
       Car C: 60 miles

    3 5 miles

    4 1.15 p.m.

    5 1.30 p.m.

    6 (a) 90 miles   (b) 90 miles

    7 1.30 p.m.

    8 Car B passed car C (stopped)

    9 40 m.p.h.

Section D (p 16)

    1 (a) Between 33 and 40 minutes
       (b) Between 10 and 20 minutes
       (c) Between 20 and 30 minutes

    2

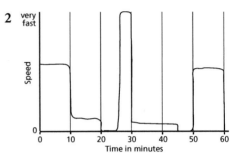

    3 Long jump (he speeds up quickly, carries
       on at the same speed for a short while,
       and then comes to a dead stop).

Working with rules

Pupils often find that using a flow diagram helps them when beginning to learn how to change the subject of a simple formula. This unit encourages them to use the flow diagram method although it does eventually have its limitations (for example, in later work when the subject appears twice). You may prefer to use the balancing method at this stage (this method is covered in our Key Stage 4 material).

p 37	**A** Solving equations	
p 38	**B** From formula to equation	
p 39	**C** Inverse rules	Rearranging simple linear formulas
p 41	**D** Using brackets	
p 42	**E** Formulas with several letters	

> **Practice booklet** pages 17 to 19

A Solving equations (p 37)

This section revises solving simple linear equations and extends to solving equations that involve division.

◊ Both methods for solving the simple equation $\frac{n}{4} + 1 = 6$ (balancing and flow diagram) are shown on the page. Pupils can compare these methods and use both methods to solve some more equations.

Unless you intend to use balancing throughout (or give pupils the choice), ask pupils to use the flow diagram method for questions A1 to A3 as a preparation for section C.

B From formula to equation (p 38)

As a lead-in to rearranging, pupils form equations from formulas and solve them to find unknown values.

B3 You may wish to extend this question and ask pupils to find the value of n for a variety of values of m. This should help to emphasise the inverse process and prepare the ground for the discussion at the beginning of the next section.

C **Inverse rules** (p 39)

◊ In the reversed flow diagram on the page, appropriate expressions are placed in the gaps to help pupils form the final expression. Some pupils may find it easier to produce the following as the reversed flow diagram and 'read off' the expression for n from the diagram.

Pattern number   Number of matches

Use the final rearranged formula to work out the pattern number for various numbers of matches and discuss how this relates to question B3 from the previous section. Check the results by using the original formula.

You may wish to include self-inverse rules such as $n = 10 - m$. A flow diagram approach can be used with 'subtract from 10' undoing itself but a balancing approach is generally found to be the most straightforward way of dealing with these.

D **Using brackets** (p 41)

E **Formulas with several letters** (p 42)

◊ Firstly, pupils can try to decide what the letters in each formula could stand for (various lengths, area of the rectangle and perimeter of the triangle). Then they can go on to try to rearrange these formulas as suggested.

Emphasise that when a formula uses more than two letters there are various ways that you can rearrange it and that the single letter in front of the equals sign (written from left to right) is called the subject of the formula.

A **Solving equations** (p 37)

A1 (a) $n = 7$ (b) $p = 9$ (c) $m = 3.5$
      (d) $k = 3.2$

A2 (a) $n = 6$ (b) $m = 9$ (c) $p = 24$
      (d) $x = 6$ (e) $x = 50$ (f) $y = 24$
      (g) $z = 30$ (h) $w = 36$

A3 (a) $x = 1.4$ (b) $y = 10$ (c) $z = 6$
      (d) $p = 21$ (e) $m = 1.5$ (f) $n = 45$
      (g) $k = 5$ (h) $h = 32$

B **From formula to equation** (p 38)

B1 (a) 180 mm or 18 cm
      (b) $7d + 40 = 320$, $d = 40$
      (c) $d = 50$

B2 (a) $\frac{w}{2} + 1 = 10$, $w = 18$

(b) $w = 28$

B3 (a) 22 matches

(b) $6n - 2 = 112$, $n = 19$ so pattern 19 uses 112 matches

(c) $n = 28$

ℂ Inverse rules (p 39)

C1 (a)
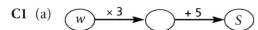

(b) (i)
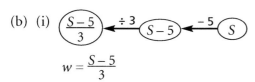

$$w = \frac{S - 5}{3}$$

(ii) 16 walkers

C2 (a)
$N \xrightarrow{\times 5} \bigcirc \xrightarrow{-3} P$

(b)
$\boxed{\frac{P + 3}{5}} \xleftarrow{\div 5} \boxed{P + 3} \xleftarrow{+ 3} P$

$$N = \frac{P + 3}{5}$$

(c) (i) 6   (ii) 20   (iii) 2.6

C3 (a) $N = \frac{P - 1}{2}$ (b) $N = \frac{P - 3}{4}$

(c) $N = \frac{P + 1}{5}$ (d) $N = \frac{P + 3}{7}$

(e) $N = \frac{P - 2}{3}$ (f) $N = \frac{P + 9}{10}$

C4 (a) 19 dots

(b) (i) $n = \frac{d + 1}{2}$ (ii) Pattern 67

C5 (a) 42   (b) 402   (c) $c = 4t + 2$

(d) (i) $t = \frac{c - 2}{4}$ (ii) 14

C6 (a) 124   (b) $c = 6t + 4$

(c) (i) $t = \frac{c - 4}{6}$ (ii) 9

C7 (a)
$x \xrightarrow{+ 3} \bigcirc \xrightarrow{\div 2} y$

(b) (i)
$\boxed{2y - 3} \xleftarrow{- 3} \boxed{2y} \xleftarrow{\times 2} y$

$x = 2y - 3$

(ii) 37

C8 (a) $p = 3q - 1$ (b) $p = 2q + 3$

(c) $p = 5q + 1$

𝔻 Using brackets (p 41)

D1 (a) $N = \frac{S}{3} - 4$ (b) $N = \frac{S}{5} + 1$

(c) $N = \frac{S}{2} + 6$

D2 (a) $x = 3(y + 5)$ (b) $x = 2(y - 1)$
(c) $x = 10(y + 3)$

D3 (a) $t = \frac{v}{4} - 5$ (b) $t = 4(v - 5)$

(c) $t = \frac{v}{3} + 9$ (d) $t = 5(v + 5)$

(e) $t = 7(v - 6)$ (f) $t = \frac{v}{2} + 10$

D4 (a) 400 cm or 4 m

(b) $L = 4(H + 15)$

(c) (i) $H = \frac{L}{4} - 15$

(ii) 100 cm or 1 m

D5 (a) (i) 4   (ii) 6   (iii) 11

(b) $b = \frac{w}{2} + 1$

(c) (i) $w = 2(b - 1)$ (ii) 38

𝔼 Formulas with several letters (p 42)

E1 (a) $N = P - M$ (b) $N = Q + A$

(c) $N = \frac{A}{M}$ (d) $N = \frac{B - P}{3}$

(e) $N = \frac{H + K}{6}$ (f) $N = 3(Y - M)$

(g) $N = 5(C + T)$ (h) $N = 4R - Y$

(i) $N = 8F + T$

E2 (a) $L = \dfrac{P}{2} - W$ (b) 7.8 cm

E3 (a) $a = \dfrac{y}{3} - b$ (b) $x = \dfrac{k}{4} + y$

    (c) $m = \dfrac{p+5}{t}$ (d) $a = \dfrac{v-u}{t}$

    (e) $p = 6y - q$ (f) $h = n(x+p)$

E4 (a) $N = Y - 2M$ (b) $N = P - 3Q$

    (c) $N = S + 2T$ (d) $N = 2(H - 3P)$

    (e) $N = 5B - 2Y$ (f) $N = 7P + 5Q$

E5 (a) $u = v - at$ (b) $x = ay + 2c$

    (c) $k = h + lm$

What progress have you made? (p 43)

1 (a) $25n + 350 = 475$, $n = 5$ so the pizza has 5 toppings

    (b) $n = \dfrac{C - 350}{25}$ (c) $n = 3$

2 (a) $n = \dfrac{p-5}{2}$ (b) $k = \dfrac{h}{3} - 1$

    (c) $X = 4Y + 3$ (d) $X = 4(Y + 3)$

    (e) $s = \dfrac{t-p}{5}$ (f) $h = g + 2k$

Practice booklet

Sections A and B (p 17)

1 (a) $s = 8$ (b) $t = 8$ (c) $v = 13.5$

2 (a) $a = 18$ (b) $b = 9$ (c) $c = 72$

    (d) $d = 56$

3 (a) $n = 4.5$ (b) $m = 8$ (c) $p = 1$

    (d) $q = 7$ (e) $r = 60$ (f) $s = 40$

4 (a) 55   (b) 16   (c) $n = 40$

5 (a) 34

    (b) $58 = 4n + 2$, the 14th pattern

    (c) $n = 37$

Sections C and D (p 18)

1 (a)

    (b)

$$N = \dfrac{T-5}{4}$$

    (c) (i) $N = 5$ (ii) $N = 11$

       (iii) $N = 10.25$

2 (a) $N = \dfrac{T+2}{3}$ (b) $N = \dfrac{T-4}{6}$

    (c) $N = \dfrac{T+5}{9}$ (d) $N = \dfrac{T-8}{2}$

3 (a) 41   (b) $n = \dfrac{d+4}{5}$

    (c) The 31st pattern

4 (a) 20   (b) $c = 2t + 4$

    (c) $t = \dfrac{c-4}{2}$ (d) 19

5 (a) $t = 6s + 2$ (b) $t = 4s - 6$

    (c) $t = 7s - 3$

6 (a) $N = \dfrac{R}{2} - 5$ (b) $N = \dfrac{R}{3} + 1$

    (c) $N = \dfrac{R}{5} - 2$

7 (a) $b = 2(a + 3)$ (b) $b = 5(a - 4)$

    (c) $b = 8(a - 7)$

Section E (p 19)

1 (a) $N = T - X$ (b) $N = R + C$

    (c) $N = \dfrac{P}{A}$ (d) $N = \dfrac{Q+P}{4}$

    (e) $N = 4(Y - X)$ (f) $N = 2Z + C$

2 (a) $v = \dfrac{d}{5} - u$ (b) 6 m/s

3 (a) $n = \dfrac{y}{5} - x$ (b) $n = \dfrac{a+b}{3}$

    (c) $n = q(p - 8)$ (d) $n = 4c - s$

    (e) $n = ce + 3d$ (f) $n = \dfrac{g-h}{k}$

Review 1 (p 44)

1 B, A, E

2 (a) $15n - 5$ (b) $x^2 + 5x$ (c) $y - y^2$

3 (a)

	$1\frac{1}{8}$	
	$\frac{3}{4}$	$\frac{3}{8}$	
$\frac{1}{2}$	$\frac{1}{4}$	$\frac{1}{8}$

    (b)

	$1\frac{8}{15}$	
	$\frac{7}{10}$	$\frac{5}{6}$	
$\frac{1}{5}$	$\frac{1}{2}$	$\frac{1}{3}$

4 A

5 (a) $\frac{1}{8}$ (b) $\frac{1}{9}$ (c) $\frac{1}{10}$ (d) $\frac{1}{4}$

6 $2n$

7 (a) 32

    (b) $c = 6t + 2$

    (c) (i) $t = \dfrac{c-2}{6}$ (ii) 9

8 16

9 (a) $n = 6p + 1$

    (b) $n = \dfrac{p}{2} - 5$ or $n = \dfrac{p-10}{2}$

    (c) $n = 4(p-1)$ or $n = 4p - 4$

10 (a) $48\,\text{cm}^3$ (b) $108\,\text{cm}^2$ (c) 1

11 (a) $6(n+2)$ (b) $3(2n-3)$

    (c) $n(6+n)$

12 $36\,\text{m}^2$

Mixed questions 1 (Practice booklet p 20)

1 (a) The pupil's cross-sections, such as

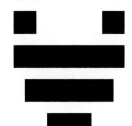

    (b) 2

2 (a) $n^2 + 5n$ (b) $15n + 5$

3 (a) $43.75\,\text{cm}^3$ (b) $405\,\text{cm}^3$

4 $5(n-3)$ and $5n - 15$

5 (a) $\frac{1}{8}$ (b) $\frac{1}{15}$ (c) $\frac{2}{21}$ (d) $\frac{2}{3}$

6 (a) $7(n+3)$ (b) $3(3n-2)$

    (c) $n(n-8)$ (d) $n(5+n)$

7 A cylinder

8 The pupil's graph, such as

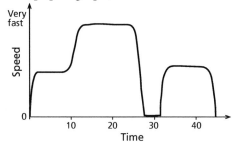

9 (a) $\frac{1}{4}$ (b) $\frac{5}{8}$ (c) $\frac{2}{3}$ (d) $\frac{1}{2}$

10 (a) $14\,\text{cm}^2$ and $30\,\text{cm}^2$

    (b) $42\,\text{cm}^2$ (c) $s = 4n + 2$

    (d) $n = \dfrac{s-2}{4}$ (e) 37 cubes

11 (a) $2x$ (b) $\dfrac{x}{3}$ (c) $\dfrac{a+1}{2}$

    (d) $\dfrac{2b-5}{6}$

12 (a) $x = 3(y-5)$ (b) $x = \dfrac{y}{6} + 5$

    (c) $x = 7y - 5$

13 $\frac{2}{5}$

6 Circumference of a circle

Essential

Different-sized cylindrical cans, thin strips of paper 40 cm or more long, scissors

Practice booklet pages 22 to 24

A   How many times? (p 46)

Cylindrical objects (tins etc.)
Thin strips of paper 40 cm or more long

◊   The section begins with a short demonstration that the circumference of a cylindrical object is a little bit more than 3 times its diameter. You can demonstrate this yourself, or involve the pupils in doing it as an experiment.

◊   Some schools made graphs relating circumference to diameter by sticking their circumference strips on to a sheet of coloured paper. A straight line graph through the origin indicates constant proportion.

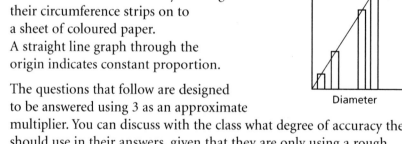

The questions that follow are designed to be answered using 3 as an approximate multiplier. You can discuss with the class what degree of accuracy they should use in their answers, given that they are only using a rough method.

B   Finding the diameter and radius (p 47)

C Becoming more accurate (p 49)

π is introduced, together with the idea of obtaining greater accuracy.

◊ In C1, if possible, pupils should be allowed to work out for themselves that the value in the second column is obtained by dividing the circumference by the diameter.

◊ If pupils do not have a π key on their calculator they can use 3.142.

◊ You can draw attention to the fact that, as so often in mathematics, from the simple definition of a circle ('all the points a given distance from a fixed point') mathematicians have derived a property (the multiplier π) that turns out to be important for advanced work in the subject. Pupils are often fascinated by the fact that the search for more decimal places for π is unending.

D Calculating diameter and radius (p 52)

D2 This question highlights a common error and is worth discussing as a class.

A How many times? (p 46)

Answers close to these are acceptable.

A1 (a) 21 cm   (b) 30 cm   (c) 18 cm

A2 (a) 45 cm   (b) 24 cm   (c) 69 cm

A3 (a) 12 cm   (b) 15 cm   (c) 7.5 cm

A4 6 cm

A5 66 cm

A6 12 cm

A7 90 m

B Finding the diameter and radius (p 47)

Answers close to these are acceptable.

B1 20 cm

B2 7 cm

B3 16 cm

B4 12 cm

B5 11 m

B6 1.5 cm

B7 380 m

B8 8000 miles

B9 7 cm

B10 1 m

B11 190 paces

B12 (a) About 2 m   (b) About 20 m
(c) About 6 m

B13 90 m

C Becoming more accurate (p 49)

C1 Answers may differ slightly from these.

Diameter	⎯ ×? ⟩→	Circumference
4 cm	3.15	12.6 cm
6 cm	3.15	18.9 cm
8 cm	3.14	25.1 cm
10 cm	3.14	31.4 cm
12 cm	3.14	37.7 cm
14 cm	3.14	44.0 cm

C2 (a) 13.8 cm   (b) 10.7 cm   (c) 8.2 cm
     (d) 5.7 cm   (e) 2.8 cm   (f) 6.6 cm

C3 (a) 2.6 cm   (b) 8.2 cm

C4 (a) 11.9 cm   (b) 8.8 cm   (c) 22.6 cm
     (d) 5.0 cm   (e) 37.1 cm

C5 (a) 20.1 cm   (b) 80.4 cm   (c) 33.0 cm
     (d) 145.8 cm   (e) 47.8 cm   (f) 95.5 cm

C6 The measured diameter, and hence the circumference, may differ from these values slightly.
     (a) Diameter = 2.7 cm
         Circumference = 8.5 cm
     (b) Diameter = 2.5 cm
         Circumference = 7.9 cm
     (c) Diameter = 0.9 cm
         Circumference = 2.8 cm
     (d) Diameter = 3.9 cm
         Circumference = 12.3 cm

Ⓓ Calculating diameter and radius
(p 52)

D1 (a) 1.6 cm   (b) 2.3 cm   (c) 2.7 cm
     (d) 3.1 cm

D2 The sequence is not correct.
It should be either

or

D3 (a) 10.7 cm   (b) 23.2 cm   (c) 7.1 cm
     (d) 16.9 cm   (e) 1.5 cm

D4 6.4 cm

D5 (a) P   (b) Q

D6 1.69 m

What progress have you made? (p 53)

   1 Diameter = 3 cm, radius = 1.5 cm

   2 6283 m (or an answer close to this)

---

   3 17.6 cm

   4 50 m further (inner circumference = 628.3 m, outer circumference = 678.6 m)

   5 11.8 cm

   6 15.9 m

Practice booklet

Sections A and B (p 22)

   1 (a) 15 cm   (b) 36 cm   (c) 51 cm

   2 (a) 96 cm   (b) 72 cm   (c) 48 cm

   3 66 m

   4 90 kerbstones

   5 (a) 13.2 m   (b) 1320 m

   6

Type of tree	Diameter	Radius
Oak	0.4 m	0.2 m
Silver birch	0.1 m	0.05 m
Horse chestnut	0.7 m	0.35 m
Yew	1.4 m	0.7 m
Beech	0.8 m	0.4 m

Section C (p 23)

   1 (a) 37.7 cm   (b) 26.4 cm   (c) 31.4 cm
       (d) 23.2 cm   (e) 51.8 cm

   2 23.6 cm

   3 (a) 44.0 cm   (b) 47.1 cm   (c) 94.2 cm
       (d) 2.5 cm   (e) 235.6 cm   (f) 565.5 cm

   4 15.7 m

Section D (p 24)

   1 (a) 7.2 cm
       (b) (i) 8.1 cm   (ii) 9.8 cm   (iii) 11.3 cm

   2 (a) 2.9 cm   (b) 8.8 cm   (c) 1.2 cm
       (d) 40.6 cm

   3 (a) 1754 km   (b) 14 km

7 Clue-sharing

Essential

Sheets 135, 255, 256, 257
Scissors

Practice booklet pages 25 and 26

Ⓐ Solving the puzzles (p 54)

◊ The puzzles can be used broadly in three ways.

- Pupils work in small groups. Clue cards are dealt out (pupils may receive different numbers of cards) and pupils look only at their own cards to begin with. This stimulates participation by requiring all pupils to consider the relevance of their own clues. They can begin by revealing what they consider to be their most 'useful' clue to the rest of the group. They continue revealing clues until the puzzle is solved. Alternatively, only the person who gets the card is allowed to see it, so they have to tell others the clues on their cards.
- Pupils work in pairs (with the clue cards visible to both or revealing clues one at a time).
- Pupils work singly.

Some may find it helps to make pencil notes on a sketch of the game board, listing alternatives and rubbing out when they realise they are on a false trail. If they do this, they must remember that numbers have to be chosen from the set specified and each number may only be used once.

The 'Three by three' puzzle is much easier to solve if 1 (2^0) is not regarded as a power of 2 here. 'Powers of 2' at this stage are generally taken as the powers of 2 that can be written as 2^n where $n = 1, 2, 3 \ldots$

'I found this excellent and enjoyed it. I think it is a unit to dip into as an interlude between other units and I will re-use it this way.'

'This proved to be an enjoyable chapter for me as well as the pupils. They had great fun doing the puzzles although some found them difficult. They enjoyed making their own as well.'

Ⓑ Inventing and trying out your own puzzles (p 54)

◊ This can provide a supply of puzzles for other groups.

'Enjoyable activity – produced some good display work.'

Section A (p 54)

Square puzzle 1

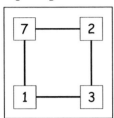

Square puzzle 2

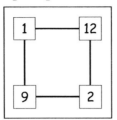

Square puzzle 3

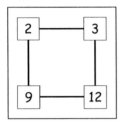

Pairs

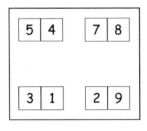

Three by three

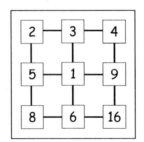

Practice booklet

Sections A and B (p 25)

1 (a) 2, 3, 5, 7, 11, 13, 17, 19
  (b) 12, 18, 24, 30, 36
  (c) 1, 2, 3, 4, 6, 9, 12, 18, 36
  (d) 1, 4, 9, 16, 25, 36, 49, 64
  (e) 31, 37, 41, 43, 47

2 Sue's puzzle

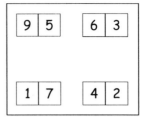

Ravi's puzzle

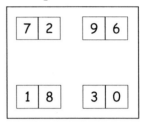

3 Daniel's puzzle

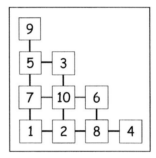

4
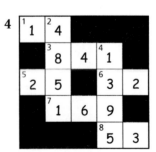

8 Enlargement

Essential	**Optional**
Sheets 258, 259, 260	Tracing paper
Practice booklet pages 27 to 29	

Ⓐ **Enlargement from a centre** (p 55)

Pupils revise enlarging a shape using the 'ray' method and also find scale factors and centres of enlargement.

> Sheets 258, 259
> Optional: Tracing paper

◊ Inaccuracies seem to arise by measuring to the nearest millimetre. For example, to the nearest millimetre, CD = 1.7 cm and C′D′ = 5.2 cm but 1.7 × 3 = 5.1. Discuss why this happens and emphasise that it doesn't mean anything has 'gone wrong'.

◊ Tracing to compare angles avoids the usual errors being picked up by an angle measurer.

◊ Discuss how you could find the centre of enlargement and scale factor where only the shape and its image are shown. Ask pupils to draw a full size copy of the diagram below where rectangle A has been enlarged to give rectangle A′.

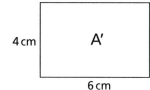

Pupils could draw these rectangles in different relative positions and look at where the centre of enlargement is each time.

A3 Pupils may realise that with a grid they can use the ray method to find the image of one point only and then use the grid to draw the complete enlarged shape. This is of course a perfectly acceptable method but encourage pupils to use the ray method to check the position of at least one more point.

Ⓑ **Using coordinates** (p 56)

Sheet 260

ℂ **Scale factors** (p 58)

◊ By the end of your discussion, pupils should see that there are essentially two ways to work out the scale factor: by comparing corresponding lengths on the 'rays' (e.g. OA'/OA) or by comparing corresponding lengths on the shapes (e.g. A'B'/AB).

The scale factor of the enlargement is 1.6 although measuring to the nearest millimetre will not give this exactly for B'C'/BC or OB'/OB.

Ⓐ **Enlargement from a centre** (p 55)

A1 Enlarged shapes on sheet 258

A2 (a) 124°   (b) 15.1 cm

A3 (a), (b), (c) Enlarged shapes on sheet 259

  (d) (i) 2

    (ii) Marked centre of enlargement

Ⓑ **Using coordinates** (p 56)

B1 (a), (b), (d)

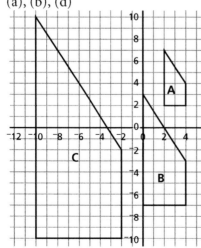

  (c) (i) Perimeter of pupil's shape: on $\frac{1}{2}$ cm squared paper this is 6.3 cm and on 1 cm squared paper this is 12.6 cm.

    (ii) Double the perimeter in part (i): on $\frac{1}{2}$ cm squared paper this is 12.6 cm and on 1 cm squared paper this is 25.2 cm.

  (e) (i) 2   (ii) (10, ⁻4)

B2

	Centre of enlargement	Scale factor
(a)	(3, 5)	2
(b)	(⁻8, 2)	3
(c)	(⁻3, 7)	2.5
(d)	(⁻1, 7)	3
(e)	(8, 4)	2
(f)	(6, 5)	1.5

B3 (a), (b)

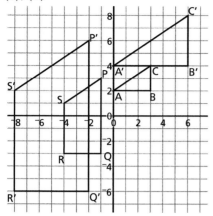

(a) (iii)

Coordinates of original shape	Coordinates of image
A (0, 2)	A′ **(0, 4)**
B (3, 2)	B′ **(6, 4)**
C (3, 4)	C′ **(6, 8)**

(b) (iii)

Coordinates of original shape	Coordinates of image
P (⁻1, 3)	P′ **(⁻2, 6)**
Q (⁻1, ⁻3)	Q′ **(⁻2, ⁻6)**
R (⁻4, ⁻3)	R′ **(⁻8, ⁻6)**
S (⁻4, 1)	S′ **(⁻8, 2)**

(c) X′ (6, 2), Y′ (8, ⁻2), Z′ (0, ⁻8)

B4 (a)

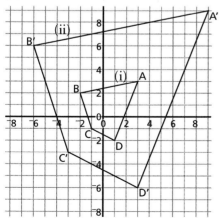

(iii)

Coordinates of original shape	Coordinates of image
A (3, 3)	A′ **(9, 9)**
B (⁻2, 2)	B′ **(⁻6, 6)**
C (⁻1, ⁻1)	C′ **(⁻3, ⁻3)**
D (1, ⁻2)	D′ **(3, ⁻6)**

(b) F′ (9, 3), G′ (12, 15), H′ (6, ⁻15)

B5 P′ (8, 4), Q′ (12, 28), R′ (⁻20, 8)

B6 K (2, 3), L (4, 1), M (⁻1, ⁻6)

*B7 (a), (b)

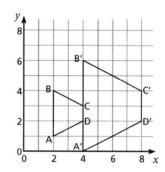

(c)

Coordinates of original shape	Coordinates of image
A (2, 1)	A′ **(4, 0)**
B (2, 4)	B′ **(4, 6)**
C (4, 3)	C′ **(8, 4)**
D (4, 2)	D′ **(8, 2)**

(d) The pupil's version of the rule that the image of (x, y) is (2x, 2y − 2) or (2x, 2(y − 1))

ℂ **Scale factors** (p 58)

C1 (a) PQ = 1.5 cm, P′Q′ = 3.3 cm (b) 2.2

C2 (a) AB = 1.6 cm, A′B′ = 4 cm
Scale factor is 2.5

(b) QR = 2.5 cm, Q′R′ = 3 cm
Scale factor is 1.2

(c) OF = 1 cm, OF′ = 3.4 cm
Scale factor is 3.4

(d) OY = 3.4 cm, OY′ = 5.1 cm
Scale factor is 1.5

C3 1.6

C4 (a) 1.5 (b) 1.5

What progress have you made? (p 60)

1 (a), (b), (c)

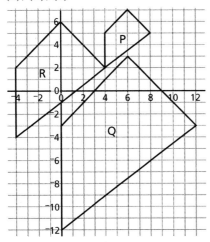

  (d) (i) 1.5 (ii) (⁻12, 12)

2 A′ (12, 2), B′ (⁻2, 8), C′ (0, 14)

3 (a) 2.5 (b) 8.25 cm (c) 65°

Practice booklet

Sections A and B (p 27)

1 (a) 37° (b) 21.6 cm

2 (a), (b), (c)

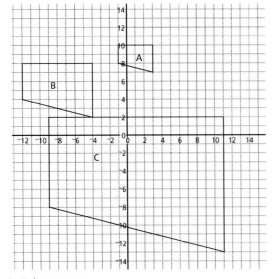

(d) (i) 2.5 (ii) (⁻14, 12)

3 P′ (6, 9), Q′ (15, ⁻6), R′ (⁻9, 3)

*4 (a), (b)

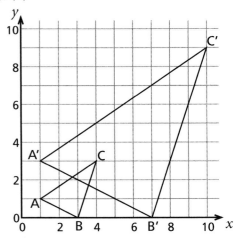

(c)

Coordinates of original shape	Coordinates of image
A (1, 1)	A′ (1, 3)
B (3, 0)	B′ (7, 0)
C (4, 3)	C′ (10, 9)

(d) The pupil's version of the rule that the image of (x, y) is $(3x - 2, 3y)$

Section C (p 28)

1 3

2 (a) AB = 2.5 cm, A′B′ = 3.5 cm
     Scale factor is 1.4

  (b) FG = 1.5 cm, F′G′ = 3.9 cm
     Scale factor is 2.6

  (c) OJ = 2.7 cm, OJ′ = 5.4 cm
     Scale factor is 2

  (d) OP = 1.8 cm, OP′ = 4.5 cm
     Scale factor is 2.5

3 $\dfrac{OZ'}{OZ} = \dfrac{OX'}{OX} = \dfrac{Z'Y'}{ZY} = 2$

⑨ Over to you

These are the 'bare bones' of the answers: pupils should include working and explanations.

1 (a) They inherit vases worth £46 + £19, £27 + £38 and £23 + £42.

   (b) Jane also inherits the vase worth £19.

2 (a) 3 journeys

   (b) The pupil's solution, for example:
630 kg + 270 kg + 100 kg
460 kg + 380 kg + 150 kg
240 kg + 290 kg + 140 kg + 310 kg

3 A: 6, B: 18, C: 1, D: 2

4 36 and 29

5 A: £24, B: £14, C: £9

6 23

7 1.5 metres

8 The shares are:
46 g + 18 g + 15 g
39 g + 26 g + 14 g
36 g + 22 g + 21 g

9 $a = 3.2$ $b = 1.3$

10 Alan, Bharat, Carol, Sadia, Kevin, Pat

⑩ Straight-line graphs

Pupil's draw graphs from algebraic equations, given in explicit and implicit form. They are introduced to the link between the equation of a graph of a straight line, its gradient and its y-intercept. Fractional gradients are not considered and neither are graphs where the scales on the x and y axes are different.

T	p 63	**A** Connections	Equations connecting variables in a table
T	p 64	**B** From equation to graph	Drawing the graph, in all four quadrants, of an equation given in explicit form
	p 66	**C** Gradient and intercept	Linking the gradient and y-intercept to the equation of a graph (positive integer gradient)
T	p 67	**D** From graph to equation	Deducing the equation of a straight line by considering the gradient and y-intercept
	p 68	**E** Sloping down	Negative integer gradients
T	p 71	**F** Implicit equations	Graphs where equations are written in implicit form such as $x + y = 5$

Essential	**Optional**
Sheets 261, 262	Graphic calculator or graph-plotting program
Practice booklet pages 30 to 33	

𝔸 **Connections** (p 63)

Pupils have previously found the connection between pairs of values in a table. This section revises that skill and extends it to examples that involve negative numbers.

◊ In most of the tables, the x values in each table increase by 1 each time so the first differences match the coefficient of x. This is not true of table R in A2 and you may wish to include an example like this in your introduction.

◊ You may wish to make the point that in calling, say, $y = 2x + 1$ an 'equation' we mean something very different from a statement like $2x + 1 = 7$, where a single value of x is to be found. You can make the point (here or during the work on graphs) that $y = 2x + 1$ is an example of a function: an important feature of a function is that for any given value of the input, x, a single value of the output, y, is obtained. By convention, when graphing a function, the input value is on the horizontal axis.

B From equation to graph (p 64)

This section revises drawing graphs of equations of the form $y = mx + c$ and extends to equations of the form $x = c$ or $y = c$.

◊ Once some integer coordinates have been plotted, ask pupils to find some values of y for some non-integer values of x and plot them too. Ask pupils if they feel sure that all the points that fit the equation lie on a straight line. It is not obvious to many that equations of the form $y = mx + c$ always give rise to straight line graphs (although many pupils will be happy to accept it) and some may feel more certain of this at the end of the unit after considering gradient and y-intercept.

◊ Clearly you only need two points to plot a straight line but a third allows a check to be made. Emphasise that calculating only two or three points will only work for straight lines.

B3, B4, B5 Giving the equations of lines parallel to the axes is often difficult for pupils. You might well wish to introduce such lines in your introduction to this section.

C Gradient and intercept (p 66)

Sheets 261, 262
Optional: Graphic calculator or graph-plotting program

◊ A graphic calculator or graph-plotting program can be used to confirm findings.

D From graph to equation (p 67)

◊ Discuss and summarise pupils' conclusions from their work in section C. Pupils now can write down the equation of a straight line once they have found the gradient and y-intercept. Once they have decided the line at the top of page 67 has the equation $y = 4x - 3$ they should check this equation fits a few coordinates of points on the line.

E Sloping down (p 68)

F Implicit equations (p 71)

◊ By the end of the discussion pupils should be able to draw up tables of values directly from the equations and hence graph them. They can also rearrange the equations to make y the subject and hence 'read off' the gradient and y-intercept.

Ⓐ **Connections** (p 63)

A1 D ($y = 3x + 1$)

A2 (a) 1, S; 2, T; 3, Q; 4, R

(b) $y = 2x + 4$

Ⓑ **From equation to graph** (p 64)

B1 (a)

x	y
-2	-1
0	3
2	7
4	11

(b), (c), (d)   Straight line through the points (-2, -1) and (4, 11) labelled with the equation $y = 2x + 3$

B2 (a) Graph of $y = x + 5$

(b) Graph of $y = x$

(c) Graph of $y = 4x + 3$

(d) Graph of $y = 3x - 4$

B3 (a) Five points of the form $(x, 4)$

(b) C ($y = 4$)

B4 (a) Five points of the form $(1, y)$

(b) E ($x = 1$)

B5 A: $y = 3$; B: $x = 3$; C: $y = -5$; D: $x = -6$

B6 (a) Graph of $y = x + 2$

(b) Graph of $y = 2$

(c) Graph of $x = -2$

(d) Graph of $y = x - 2$

Ⓒ **Gradient and intercept** (p 66)

C1 (a) 4   (b) 1   (c) 3

C2 A

(a) 1

(b) Completed table with three 1s in the second column

(c) (i) Graph of $y = x + 3$ (ii) 1

(d) The gradients are all 1.

(e) The equations all begin '$y = x$ …'

B

(a) Graph of $y = 2x$

(b) Completed table with four 2s in the second column

(c) The gradients are all 2.

(d) The equations all begin '$y = 2x$ …'

C3 (a) Graph of $y = 3x - 2$

(b) Completed table with 2, 3, 4, 5 in the second column

(c) The pupil's description such as: 'The gradient gives the number that x is multiplied by'.

(d) Completed table with -5, -2, 1, 9 in the second column

(e) The pupil's description such as: 'The y-intercept gives the number that is added to the expression involving x.'

C4 (a) 2   (b) 6   (c) 3   (d) 1

C5 (a) A and D ($y = 3x + 4$ and $y = 3x - 1$)

(b) A and C ($y = 3x + 4$ and $y = 5x + 4$)

Ⓓ **From graph to equation** (p 67)

D1 (a) 2   (b) 1   (c) $y = 2x + 1$

D2 (a) 3   (b) -1   (c) $y = 3x - 1$

D3 (a) Line through (1, 4) and (3, 8)

(b) $y = 2x + 2$

D4 (a) (i) Line through (-1, -5) and (2, 7)

(ii) $y = 4x - 1$

(b) (i) Line through (0, 3) with gradient 4

(ii) $y = 4x + 3$

D5 (a) (i) Line through (1, 4) and (3, 10)

(ii) $y = 3x + 1$

(b) (i) Line through (2, 1) with gradient 3

(ii) $y = 3x - 5$

E Sloping down (p 68)

E1 (a)

x	y
-2	5
0	3
2	1
4	-1

(b), (c), (d) Line through (⁻2, 5) and (4, ⁻1) labelled $y = 3 - x$.

E2 (a) Graph of $y = 4 - 2x$

(b) Graph of $y = 2 - 3x$

(c) Graph of $y = 6 - x$

(d) Graph of $y = {}^-4x + 7$

E3 (a) ⁻2

(b) Completed table with ⁻1, ⁻2, ⁻3, ⁻4 in the second column and 10, 8, 6, ⁻1 in the third column

(c) The pupil's description such as: 'The size of the gradient gives the number in front of x either negative or subtracted.'

(d) The pupil's description such as: 'The y-intercept gives the number that is added to the expression involving x or that the expression involving x is subtracted from.'

E4 (a) (i) ⁻1 (ii) 7
(iii) $y = 7 - x$ or $y = {}^-x + 7$

(b) $y = 4 - 3x$ or $y = {}^-3x + 4$

E5 (a) Line through (⁻1, 6) and (5, 0)

(b) $y = 5 - x$ or $y = {}^-x + 5$

E6 (a) (i) Line through (1, 4) and (4, ⁻2)

(ii) $y = 6 - 2x$ or $y = {}^-2x + 6$

(b) (i) Line through (1, 0) with gradient ⁻2

(ii) $y = 2 - 2x$ or $y = {}^-2x + 2$

E7 A: $y = x + 3$ B: $y = 2x - 2$

C: $y = 3 - 2x$ or $y = {}^-2x + 3$

D: $y = 4 - x$ or $y = {}^-x + 4$

E: $y = {}^-2 - x$ or $y = {}^-x - 2$

F Implicit equations (p 71)

F1 (a) Graph of $x + y = 8$

(b) Graph of $y - x = 6$

(c) Graph of $y - 2x = 3$

(d) Graph of $y + 3x = 9$

F2 (a) Completed table with 4, 3, 2, 1, 0, ⁻1 in the bottom row

(b) Identical table to (a)

(c) The values in both tables are the same with the pupil's explanation such as: 'The equations $x + y = 3$ and $y = 3 - x$ are rearrangements of each other.'

F3 (a) $y = x + 5$ or $y = 5 + x$

(b) 1   (c) 5

F4 (a) $y = 5 - 2x$ (b) ⁻2   (c) 5

F5 B and D ($y = 2x + 4$ and $y - 2x = 7$)

F6 (a), (b) Graphs of $y = x + 4$ and $x + y = 2$

(c) (⁻1, 3)

(d) Graph of $y = x - 2$; (2, 0)

(e) Graph of $y = 8 - x$ with its equation

What progress have you made? (p 72)

1 B ($y = 3x - 1$)

2 (a) (i) 3   (ii) 1   (iii) ⁻3

(b) Graph of $y = 2x - 3$

3 (a) B ($y = 2x + 3$)

(b) C ($y = 3x + 5$)

(c) D ($y = 3 - 5x$)

4 (a) 1   (b) ⁻2   (c) $y = x - 2$

5 (a) (i) Line through (3, 10) and (⁻1, ⁻2)

(ii) $y = 3x + 1$

(b) (i) Line through $(0, {}^-4)$ with gradient 3

(ii) $y = 3x - 4$

6 (a) Graph of $y + 2x = 7$

(b) A and D $(y = {}^-2x + 1$ and $y = 8 - 2x)$

Practice booklet

Sections A and B (p 30)

1 (a) A: $y = 2x + 2$ B: $y = x - 2$
D: $y = 3x - 1$

(b) $y = x + 5$

2 (a)

x	y
-2	-8
0	-2
2	4
4	10

(b), (c), (d)   Line through $({}^-2, {}^-8)$ and $(4, 10)$ labelled $y = 3x - 2$

3 (a) Graph of $y = x + 4$

(b) Graph of $y = 2x$

(c) Graph of $y = 2x - 3$

4 Graphs of
$y = 3, y = x, x = {}^-1$ and $y = x - 3$,
all on the same axes

Sections C and D (p 31)

1 (a) 2   (b) ${}^-3$ (c) $y = 2x - 3$

2 (a) 3   (b) 2   (c) $y = 3x + 2$

3 (a) (i) 4   (ii) ${}^-3$

(b) (i) 1   (ii) 7

(c) (i) 5   (ii) 1

4 (a) (i) Line through $(1, 1)$ and $(3, 5)$

(ii) $y = 2x - 1$

(b) (i) Line through $(1, {}^-2)$ with gradient 2

(ii) $y = 2x - 4$

1 (a)

x	y
-2	7
0	5
2	3
4	1

(b), (c), (d)   Line through $({}^-2, 7)$ and $(4, 1)$ $y = 5 - x$

2 (a) Graph of $y = 4 - x$

(b) Graph of $y = {}^-x$

(c) Graph of $y = 6 - 4x$

(d) Graph of $y = {}^-3x + 5$

3 (a) (i) ${}^-1$ (ii) 2   (iii) $y = 2 - x$

(b) $y = 6 - 2x$

4 (a) (i) Line through $(0, 7)$ and $(3, 1)$

(ii) $y = 7 - 2x$ or $y = {}^-2x + 7$

(b) (i) Line through $(1, 1)$ with gradient ${}^-2$

(ii) $y = 3 - 2x$ or $y = {}^-2x + 3$

Section F (p 33)

1 (a) Graph of $x + y = 5$

(b) Graph of $y - 2x = 6$

(c) Graph of $y + 2x = 4$

2 (a) $y = 3x + 2$ (b) 3   (c) 2

3 A and D; $(x + y = {}^-2$ and $y = 8 - x)$
B and C; $(y - 3x = 4$ and $y = 3x - 7)$

4 A: $y - x = 4$; B: $x + y = 3$
C: $y - 2x = {}^-3$; D: $y = 6 - 3x$

5 (a), (b)   Graph of $y = x - 1$ and $y = 1 - x$

(c) Line through $(4, 0)$ and $(0, 8)$
$y = 8 - 2x$

(d) Line through $({}^-2, 0)$ and $(0, 4)$
$y = 2x + 4$

(e) Kite

Points, lines and arcs

Essential

Counters, sheet 263
compasses, set squares, angle measurers

Practice booklet page 34 (needs compasses and angle measurer)

A Sets of points (p 73)

> Counters, sheet 263, compasses, set squares

During the initial discussion pupils could participate in placing points on the board or on an OHP. Since the idea of a locus as 'the set of all points that …' is sometimes found difficult, activities with counters can provide a good start. They also give confidence in dealing with questions where points have to fulfil more than one condition. This is a good opportunity to practise skills of estimating distances.

'Without measuring, try to place an orange counter 20 cm from the white counter. Now check with a ruler and correct the orange counter's position. Do the same with your other orange counters.'

'Place a coin so that it is less than 20 cm from the middle counter.'

'Suppose I wanted to use red paint to show all the possible places you could put a coin less than 20 cm from the middle counter. Where would I paint?

'Place a coin so it is more than 20 cm from the middle counter but less than 30 cm from it.'

'Place each green counter so that it is 15 cm from the short edge of the table.'

'Show me a point that is more than 15 cm from the short edge of the table and is less than 25 cm from the corner.'

'Suppose I wanted to use yellow paint to show all the possible points that meet those two conditions, where would I paint?

A1   You may need to revise accurate drawing of a line parallel to a given line and a given distance from it, using a set square and ruler.

Ⓑ **Accurate drawing** (p 74)

Compasses, angle measurers, set squares

B1, B2 and B7 revise SSS, SAS and ASA constructions for a triangle. B4 and B5 introduce the construction for a triangle where a right angle, hypotenuse and side are given.

Ⓐ **Sets of points** (p 73)

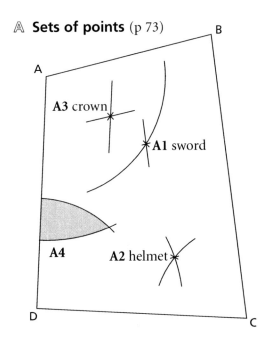

A1 (d) The sword is 9.3 m from corner B.

Ⓑ **Accurate drawing** (p 74)

B1 (a) The pupil's drawing
   (b) 6.6 cm, which is 132 cm on the real kite
   (c) 136°; the angle will be the same on the real kite.
   (d) One line of reflection symmetry, AD

B2 (a) The pupil's drawing
   (b) (i) 8.2 km   (ii) 10.6 km
      (iii) 7.1 km

B3 (a) The pupil's drawing   (b) 5.5 m

B4 (a) The pupil's drawing   (b) 3 cm
   (c) 1.5 m

B5 18 m

B6 (a) 75 km   (b) 40 km

B7 (a) The pupil's drawing
   (b) The smaller triangle: approximately 24 m^2
      The larger triangle: approximately 42 m^2
   (c) Approximately 66 m^2

What progress have you made? (p 76)

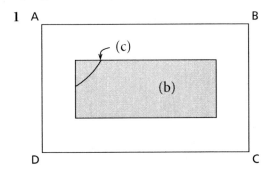

2 The pupil's diagram
The widest the bed can be is 0.8 m (80 cm).

Practice booklet

Section A (p 34)

1

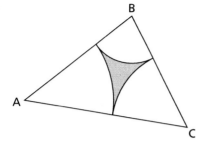

2

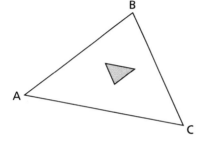

Section B (p 34)

1 (a), (b)

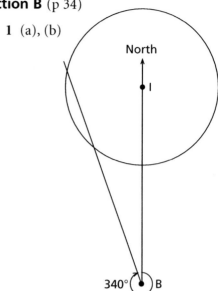

(c) Yes, for about 42 km

2 3.3 metres

⑫ Percentage problems

As in 'Percentage change' in the previous book, each percentage change is linked to a multiplier and the change worked out from that. We would strongly recommend this method as it has been found to be very successful.

The alternative method of working out the change and expressing is as a percentage of the original is not considered though, of course, it may be discussed and used. One disadvantage of this method is that the more difficult 'reverse percentage' problems which appear later in the course (work out the original amount given the final amount and the percentage change) are more difficult to solve.

p 77	**A** Review: increasing and decreasing
p 78	**B** Finding an increase as a percentage
p 79	**C** Finding a decrease as a percentage
p 80	**D** Mixed increases and decreases
p 81	**E** Mixed problems

Practice booklet pages 35 to 37

Ⓐ Review: increasing and decreasing (p 77)

Ⓑ Finding an increase as a percentage (p 78)

◊ Pairs of pupils can discuss the problems at the top of page 78. It is intended that they solve the problems by working out the multipliers and 'reading off' the increases from them.

So, for example, to find the increase from 1.40 m to 1.75 m first find the multiplier such that $1.40 \times ? = 1.75$ by dividing 1.75 by 1.4 to obtain 1.25. The increase of 25% can now be 'read off' from the multiplier.

In the third example, the multiplier is 1.276 119 402 99... and you may need to discuss how to deal with this by rounding to 1.28 to give an increase of 28%. Although it is not covered here, at this point you may wish to discuss rounding to 1.276 giving an increase of 27.6%.

C Finding a decrease as a percentage (p 79)

Finding percentage decreases by looking at multipliers is harder than finding increases as the decrease is not so 'obvious' from the multiplier.

◊ It is intended that pupils find the decrease for Emma's car by first finding the multiplier by dividing 4760 by 5600 to obtain 0.85. As this is 0.15 less than 1 it represents a decrease of 15%. Pupils will probably need to discuss a few examples before they feel confident about this method.

D Mixed increases and decreases (p 80)

E Mixed problems (p 81)

A Review: increasing and decreasing (p 77)

A1 (a) × 1.15
(b) Alastair £2.30, Siobhan £3.45

A2 (a) C (× 1.04)   (b) A (× 1.4)
(c) B (× 1.14)

A3 £19 240

A4 (a) × 0.72   (b) £3240

A5 (a) B (× 0.37)   (b) A (× 0.7)
(c) C (× 0.97)

A6 £28

A7 (a) 71 kg   (b) 29 kg

B Finding an increase as a percentage (p 78)

B1 15%

B2 8%

B3 20%

B4 (a) The pupil's answer
(b) A: Grey seal   22%
B: Bernese mountain dog   83%
C: Blue whale   53%
D: Human being   31%
E: Guernsey heifer   23%
The pupil's comment on their answer in (a)

B5 33%

B6 31%

B7 6%

B8 70%

C Finding a decrease as a percentage (p 79)

C1 (a) 0.74   (b) 26%

C2 34%

C3 40%

C4 (a) 0.36   (b) 64%

C5 (a) The pupil's answer

(b) A   25%

     B   52%

     C   57%

     D   33%

     E   15%

The pupil's comment on their answer in (a)

C6 14%

C7 6%

D Mixed increases and decreases
(p 80)

D1 74%

D2 88%

D3 74%

D4 (a) 5%   (b) 16%

D5 (a) 22%   (b) 28%

(c) The pupil's comments, for example: 'Although the number of miles travelled on average has gone up, the number of miles walked has gone down'.

D6 The number of vehicles stolen **decreased** by 32%.

D7 (a) The percentage change was 5% and this was an increase.

(b) The percentage change was 1% and this was an increase.

(c) The pupil's comments, for example: 'The increase in pupils at private schools cannot just be explained by an overall increase in pupil numbers as the increase is larger than the overall increase.'

E Mixed problems (p 81)

E1 £1.26

E2 75%

E3 8.5 g

E4 (a) 2%   (b) 741 000

E5 25%

*__E6__ (a) 31%   (b) 8%   (c) 2%

(d) (i) a decrease of 16%

     (ii) an increase of 46%

     (iii) an increase of 207%

What progress have you made? (p 82)

1   20%

2   10%

3   20%

4   27%

Practice booklet

Section B (p 35)

1   15%

2   12%

3   (a) The pupil's choice

(b)
Ready salted	15%
Salt and vinegar	47%
Cheese and onion	35%
Barbecue	31%

(c) The pupil's comment

4   6%

5   19%

Section C (p 35)

1   18%

2 1%

3 (a) The pupil's choice

(b)
Radio	18%
Television	21%
Walkman	27%
Video camera	29%

(c) The pupil's comment

4 39%

5 (a) The pupil's choice

(b) 46% (c) 57%

(d) The pupil's comment

Section D (p 36)

1 2%

2 25%

3 Butter 15% decrease
Spreads 51% increase

Section E (p 37)

1 £19 610

2 £28.29

3 61%

4 (a) The pupil's choice

(b) 56% (c) 11%

*5 (a) 53% (b) 143%

Review 2 (p 83)

1 The circumference of the cake is
$\pi \times 30 = 94.2$ (to 1 d.p.) so the ribbon
will be long enough.

2 (a) 2   (b) S

3 £26 250

4 (a) (i) A   (ii) $y = 5x$
  (b) $y = 2x - 3$

5 (a) 2   (b) 4   (c) 19

6 13%

7

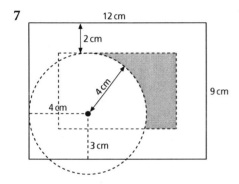

8 30%

9 3.2 cm

10 (a) Graph of $y + 2x = 8$ going through
   (0, 8) and (4, 0)
   (b) $^{-}2$

11 The maximum width is 1.34 to 1.36 m.

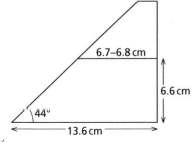

12 44%

13 (a) A: $y = 8 - x$ or $y = {}^{-}x + 8$
     B: $y = 10 - 3x$ or $y = {}^{-}3x + 10$
     C: $y = 6 + 3x$ or $y = 3x + 6$
     D: $y = 5 + 3x$ or $y = 3x + 5$

   (b) C and D

Mixed questions 2 (Practice booklet p 38)

1 (a), (b), (c), (d)

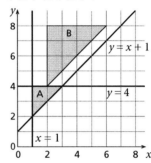

  (e) (2, 4), (2, 8) and (6, 8)

2 (a) A circle radius 5 m centred at the
     bottom of the pole
  (b) 31.4 m (to 1 d.p.)

3 A (a) 2   (b) 1   (c) $y = 2x + 1$
  B (a) 1   (b) $^{-}3$ (c) $y = x - 3$
  C (a) $^{-}1$ (b) 5   (c) $y = {}^{-}x + 5$
                              or $x + y = 5$

4 (a), (b)

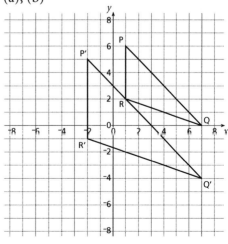

  (c) 1.5   (d) (7, 8)

5 The pupil's scale drawing, leading to
   (a) 75 km   (b) 99 km

6 12%

7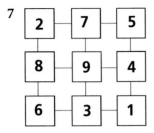

8 142 000 km

9 8%

10 (a) The pupil's accurate drawing of

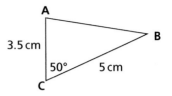

    (b) 12.3 cm

    (c) (i) The pupil's enlarged triangle
            (scale factor 3)

       (ii) 36.9 cm

      (iii) 50°

11 ⁻5

⑬ Ratio and proportion

> **Practice booklet** pages 40 and 41

Ⓐ **Single number ratios** (p 85)

Ⓑ **Ratio and direct proportion** (p 86)

◊   You could begin the discussion by revising earlier work on direct proportion where pupils saw that when two quantities are in direct proportion, multiplying one quantity up (or down) will result in the other being multiplied up (or down) by the same factor. Pupils can see that this is true for the first table but not for the second.

Then pupils can consider the ratios $\frac{b}{a}$ and $\frac{y}{x}$ as suggested.
By the end of the discussion they should see that

- since the ratios $\frac{b}{a}$ have the same value (60), b is directly proportional to a (for example, as $\frac{120}{2} = \frac{60}{1}$ then a multiplier exists to convert one fraction into the other and, as this works for any pair of fractions, then b is in direct proportion to a)

- the value of the ratio gives the multiplier in the equation $b = 60a$

- the graph of b against a is a straight line through $(0, 0)$

The value of the ratio can be linked to the gradient of the straight line. Conversely, since the ratios $\frac{y}{x}$ do not have the same value, y is not directly proportional to x. Although the graph of y against x is a straight line, it does not go through $(0, 0)$ so y is not directly proportional to x.

B2   You may wish to point out that the ratio $\frac{\text{weight}}{\text{volume}}$ is called density.

B5   Essentially, there are two ways to solve each problem, either by using the constant ratio $\frac{y}{x}$ each time or by considering multipliers across the table. For example in (a) $\frac{y}{x} = 2.5$ each time so the missing value is $2.8 \times 2.5 = 7.0$. Alternatively $\frac{2.8}{1.4} = 2$ so the missing value is $3.5 \times 2 = 7.0$. Some pupils may be ready to discuss and use alternative methods while others may find this confusing. One possible source of confusion is that while the ratios $\frac{y}{x}$ remain constant, the multipliers across the table do not.

ℂ **Using algebra** (p 88)

The methods of solution shown on the pupil's page are those that link directly with the earlier work in section B on constant ratios. However, other approaches can be considered.

The first problem can be solved as shown or by forming the equation $\frac{k}{11.2} = \frac{11}{7}$.

The second problem can be solved as shown or by forming the equation $\frac{r}{11} = \frac{63}{6}$ or by using the unitary method (working out how much red paint you need for **one** litre of yellow paint first).

𝔸 **Single number ratios** (p 85)

A1 (a) 2   (b) 1.6   (c) 0.75

A2 Square

A3 Hamster   0.2
Cat   0.1
Elephant   0.004

A4 2.4

A5 19.2

A6 (a) Fiesta pink   1.27
Passion pink   0.7
Hot pink   1.43
Baby pink   0.25

    (b) Hot pink as the ratio is highest showing the largest proportion of red

𝔹 **Ratio and direct proportion** (p 86)

B1 (a) The ratios are 1.5, 1.25, 1.17 (to 2 d.p.), 1.125

    (b) The ratios are different.

B2 (a) The ratios are all 0.8 .

    (b) The ratios are all the same.

    (c) $W = 0.8V$

    (d) 57.6 grams

B3 (a) The ratios are all 3.5 .

    (b) The ratios are all the same.

    (c) $n = 3.5t$

    (d) 119 copies

B4 (a) The ratios are all 2 so b is proportional to a and $b = 2a$.

    (b) The ratios are 3, 3, 4.33 (to 2 d.p.), 6 so b is not proportional to a.

    (c) The ratios are all 1.8 so b is proportional to a and $b = 1.8a$.

    (d) The ratios are 5, 3.67 (to 2 d.p.), 5, 6.71 (to 2 d.p.) so b is not proportional to a.

B5 (a) 7.0   (b) 36.0   (c) 0.16
    (d) 2.3   (e) 6.5   (f) 3.8

B6 (a) The line does not go through $(0, 0)$.
    (b) The pupil's ratios, e.g. $\frac{2}{1}, \frac{3}{2}, \ldots$

ℂ **Using algebra** (p 88)

C1 (a) $\frac{n}{8.6} = \frac{7.8}{1.2}$ (or $\frac{n}{7.8} = \frac{8.6}{1.2}$)

    (b) $n = 55.9$

C2 (a) $\frac{k}{18.9} = \frac{7.5}{10.5}$

       (or $\frac{k}{7.5} = \frac{18.9}{10.5}$)

    (b) $k = 13.5$

C3 100.8 litres

C4 10.5 grams

C5 8.7

What progress have you made? (p 90)

1 (a) 0.71   (b) 0.75

2 (a) The ratios are 0.23, 0.21, 0.18, 0.17
(all to 2 d.p.).

(b) The ratios are different.

3 (a) The ratios are all 1.5.

(b) The ratios are the same.

(c) $y = 1.5x$ (d) 5.1

4 (a) $\dfrac{n}{9.5} = \dfrac{8.5}{2.5}$ (or $\dfrac{n}{8.5} = \dfrac{9.5}{2.5}$)

(b) $n = 32.3$

Practice booklet

Sections A and B (p 40)

1 (a) 1.6   (b) 1.5   (c) 2.5

2 4.7

3 (a) Tropical tango   1.6
Tropical sizzler   1.7
Tropical refresher   1.4

(b) Tropical sizzler

4 (a) 0.75, 0.72, 0.7

(b) The ratios are not all the same.

5 (a) 15, 15, 15, 15

(b) All the ratios are the same.

(c) $n = 15t$

(d) 240 bottles

6 A: (a) 7.2   (b) $y = 3x$

   B: (a) 14.3   (b) $y = 6.5x$

   C: (a) 35   (b) $y = 1.2x$

   D: (a) 9.2   (b) $y = 0.25x$

Section C (p 41)

1 (a) $\dfrac{n}{6.7} = \dfrac{7.48}{4.4}$ or $\dfrac{n}{7.48} = \dfrac{6.7}{4.4}$

(b) $n = 11.39$

2 39.9 grams

⑭ Angles of a polygon

Essential	Optional
Angle measurer	Compasses
Scissors	

Practice booklet pages 42 and 43 (requires angle measurer)

A Interior angles (p 91)

> Angle measurer

◊ Two facts should emerge – that a polygon with n sides can be split into $n - 2$ triangles (so long as all the vertices of the triangles coincide with the vertices of the polygon) and that the sum of the angles of those triangles equals the sum of the angles of the polygon.

(Splitting a polygon into triangles in these ways leads to the standard result, but they are avoided here to minimise confusion.)

◊ You may need to revise the fact that the angles of a triangle add up to 180°.

◊ This approach to establishing the sum of the interior angles has been used for quadrilaterals earlier in the course. The general rule should emerge from discussion of the polygons A to D. Pupils may express it as a formula, as an arrow diagram or in words.

$$A = 180(n - 2)$$

number of sides $\longrightarrow$ $\boxed{-2}$ $\longrightarrow$ $\boxed{\times 180}$ $\longrightarrow$ sum of interior angles

A7 Pupils need to recall the sum of the angles on a straight line and the sum of the angles around a point.

B Exterior angles (p 93)

> Scissors

◊ The class can all do the exterior angles experiment or you can demonstrate it on an overhead projector. With everyone doing it, pupils see that it works for polygons of different shapes and with different numbers of sides. Be careful, however, to avoid reflex interior angles: they do not create a pointed piece of the kind needed for this demonstration to work.

For an alternative demonstration, draw a polygon on the board or OHP. Place a pencil along one of the sides; move it around the polygon, emphasising the exterior angle through which it turns at each vertex. When the pencil returns to its starting point focus discussion on what angle it has turned through and what this means for the total of the exterior angles.

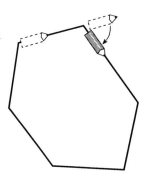

ℂ **Regular polygons** (p 95)

Angle measurer
Optional: compasses

C8 An aim of this question is to show that the angles between the spokes can also be marked with a ●. Other features may emerge – for example that the triangles are isosceles and that × is half the interior angle of the polygon.

You can discuss the symmetries of different regular polygons.

C11 This can be the basis for some work using LOGO.

𝔸 **Interior angles** (p 91)

A1 (a) 1260°
(b) The pupil's drawing and calculation

A2 (a) 1440°
(b) The pupil's drawing and calculation

A3 A (a) 5 (b) 540° (c) 115°
B (a) 6 (b) 720° (c) 100°
C (a) 8 (b) 1080° (c) 135°

A4 $a = 98°$ $b = 52°$

A5 $p = 120°$ $q = 130°$ $r = 135°$ $s = 108°$

A6 $a = 125°$ $b = 94°$ $c = 141°$ $d = 141°$

A7 $a = 70°$ $b = 110°$ $c = 70°$ $d = 102°$
$e = 120°$ $f = 70°$ $g = 120°$ $h = 140°$
$i = 110°$ $j = 90°$ $k = 130°$

A8 15

𝔹 **Exterior angles** (p 93)

B1 $a = 72°$ $b = 60°$ $c = 43°$ $d = 67°$
$e = 55°$ $f = 63°$

B2 $a = 120°$ $b = 145°$ $c = 80°$ $d = 150°$
$e = 135°$ $f = 128°$ $g = 142°$

B3 $a = 53°$ $b = 79°$ $c = 37°$

B4 $a = 59°$ $b = 78°$ $c = 109°$

ℂ **Regular polygons** (p 95)

C1 (a) 360° (b) 60°

C2 (a) 720° (b) 120°

C3

(a) Name of polygon	Number of sides	(b) Size of each exterior angle	(c) Size of each interior angle
Quadrilateral	4	90°	90°
Pentagon	5	72°	108°
Hexagon	6	60°	120°
Heptagon	7	$51\frac{3}{7}°$	$128\frac{4}{7}°$
Octagon	8	45°	135°

(d) They always add up to 180°.
This is as expected because they are angles on a straight line.

C4 (a) Exterior angle 40°, interior angle 140°

    (b) Exterior angle 18°, interior angle 162°

C5 (a) 18 (b) 15 (c) 12

C6 (a) 36° (b) 10

C7 (a) 24 (b) 40

C8 (a) 12

    (b)

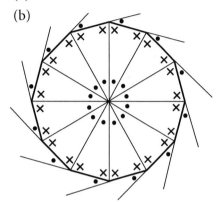

C9 (a) 36 (b) 10°

C10 (a) 24° (b) 24° (c) 156°

C11 (a) An octagon

    (b) FORWARD 20
        RIGHT   72
        FORWARD 20
        RIGHT   72
        FORWARD 20
        RIGHT   72
        FORWARD 20
        RIGHT   72
        FORWARD 20

    (c) As for (b) but with the FORWARD value doubled

C12 (a) 60°   (b) 120°   (c) 180°
     (d) 240°   (e) 300°   (f) 000°

C13 (a) 90°   (b) 160°   (c) 250°
     (d) 340°

What progress have you made? (p 98)

1 1620°

2 (a) 120°   (b) 78°

3 62°

4 (a) 12°   (b) 168°

5 (a) 6°   (b) 60

Practice booklet

Section A (p 42)

1 A (a) 6   (b) 720°   (c) 75°
   B (a) 9   (b) 1260° (c) 140°
   C (a) 8   (b) 1080° (c) 150°

2 (a) $p = 42°$ $q = 36°$ (b) $r = 110°$

3 $a = b = c = d = 135°$

4 230°

5 20

Sections B and C (p 43)

1 (a) $a = 50°$ (b) $x = 50°$
   (c) $a = 150°$ $b = 130°$ $c = 55°$
      $d = 50°$ $e = 70°$ $f = 115°$
      $g = 40°$ $h = 140°$

2 (a) 20   (b) 24   (c) 72

3 (a) (b) (c)

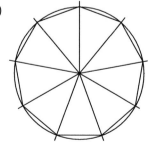

4 (a) 12°   (b) 30

5 (a) 120°   (b) 108°   (c) 12°

Using and misusing statistics

Practice booklet page 44

Ⓐ Presenting data (p 99)

Some ways of presenting data are revised and pupils are asked to choose statistical investigations in which they would be effective. Pupils can make these choices while working through the revision questions, or as part of teacher-led class discussions.

A5 While the diagram at the top of page 101 may suggest grouping prices as, say, 50–99, 100–149, … , the alternative convention, 51–100, 101–150, … is also acceptable.

Ⓑ Misleading charts and pictures (p 103)

◊ Whether a chart 'misleads' or not is to some extent subjective. A chart that distorts the relative values of quantities is misleading. One that uses a false origin correctly but tries to draw the reader's attention away from it by emphasising other features may mislead only the unwary.

◊ The first chart ('YUK Computers') is only misleading to someone who does not notice that the vertical scale starts at 2000. It would be better if this were shown by a jagged axis and broken bars.

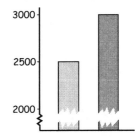

◊ The second chart distorts by making the second bar wider as well as higher than the first.

◊ Showing the pie chart at an angle makes it harder to tell the relative sizes of the slices, taking away the main reason for using such a chart. (Teachers shown this chart have come up with a surprising range of answers. The actual proportions shown are meat 30%, gravy 30% and crust 40%.)

◊ In the lottery chart the heights of the flags are in proportion to the amounts, but the different widths mislead. (A more subtle point is the lack of any reference to the different sizes of the countries shown and the size of the lottery contributions in relation to the national incomes.)

A Presenting data (p 99)

A1 (a)

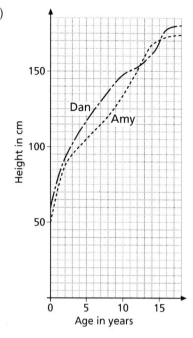

(b) Dan

(c) At age $12\frac{1}{4}$

(d) Between ages $12\frac{1}{4}$ and $15\frac{1}{4}$

(e) Amy grew most quickly between the ages of 0 and 2 years, slowing down between 3 and 4 and then growing steadily until she was 14 when her growth rate slowed again.

(f) Dan grew a little more slowly than Amy initially, and maintained a steadier rate of growth until he was 10, when the rate slowed so much that he fell behind Amy. A growth spurt at age 14 continued until he was 17, and during this time, he overtook Amy again.

A2 (a)

	Girls	Boys	Total
Candlestick	2	6	8
Faces	4	0	4
Total	6	6	12

(b) The pupil's comments such as: More pupils saw a candlestick than saw faces. None of the boys saw faces – they all saw candlesticks. $\frac{2}{3}$ of the girls saw faces.

A3 (a)

	Can smell	Cannot smell	Total
Male	59	29	88
Female	47	15	62
Total	106	44	150

(b) 67% of the males could smell the flower, which is less than the 76% of females who could smell it.

A4 Mean 14.2 m (to 1 d.p.)
Median 13.6 m
Range 5.4 m

A5 (a)

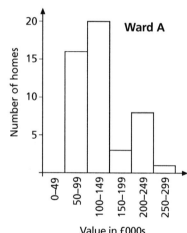

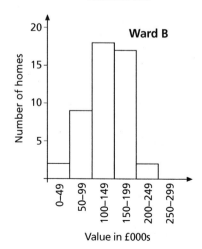

(b) Both the cheapest and most expensive homes in Ward A have higher values then the cheapest/most expensive in Ward B. However, most homes in Ward A are valued between 50 and 150 thousand pounds but most homes in Ward B are valued between 100 and 200 thousand pounds. Homes in Ward A appear to fall into two distinct groups by value, with far fewer in the middle, while in Ward B, most homes have values in the middle of the range.

(c) Ward: mean $\left(= \frac{6447}{48}\right) \approx 134$
range = 182
Ward B: mean $\left(= \frac{6418}{48}\right) \approx 134$
range = 178

The mean and range are almost the same for the two wards and so are not very useful for making comparison here.

B Misleading charts and pictures (p 103)

B1 (a) The scale does not start at zero – looks like Japan has twice the percentage of the UK, for example.

(b) The labels here are part of the bars. This makes them look disproportionate. The bars actually start some 27 mm from the left.

B2 (a) The vertical scale goes up in very uneven steps. The pictures also have disproportionate area.

(b) A classic example where the height this year may be 1.5 times last year's but the area is $1.5^2 = 2.25$ times bigger.

B3 Putting a slice at the front exaggerates its significance. 'Leisure' shows the effect of different positions well.

B4 Bembo appears to have had a more rapid rise but in fact both companies' sales have increased by a factor of about 4.

B5 The first graph does not start at zero. The second does not go up to 100%.

B6 Wages have increased from £2 million to £3 million between 2000 and 2003. Profits have increased from about £4.1 million to £5.6 million. So wages have increased by £1 million compared with £1.5 million for profits.
But the wage increase is 50%, while the profits increase is only about 37%. So the headline is not fair.

What progress have you made? (p 106)

1 The vertical scale does not start at zero. Years are not evenly spaced.

Practice booklet

Sections A and B (p 44)

1 The pupil's comment such as: A pie chart is a good way to display non-numerical data, such as the eye colours of a group of students. It is most effective where there is a small choice of possible attributes (such as eye colour).

2 (a) Chart C
(b) The bar for 2002 is wider than the bar for 2001 in chart A. The vertical scales does not start at 0 in chart B.

3 The chart shows a 'sugar lump' for each country, with the length of the lump's side being proportional to the amount of sugar produced. So, for example, the cube for the USSR has sides almost twice as long as the cube for India. However, the reader looks at their volumes, which suggest, for example, that the USSR's sugar production is almost eight times that of India which is clearly misleading.

⑯ Linear sequences

In previous work, sequences mainly arose in contexts (tile patterns, mobile designs, stitching patterns, …). Here, there are no contexts to help pupils find rules.

T	p 107 **A** Continuing sequences	Understanding what is meant by sequence, term, differences, linear sequence Describing and using rules to continue sequences
T	p 108 **B** Sequences from rules	Finding terms in a sequence by using the nth term
T	p 110 **C** Increasing linear sequences	Finding and using an expression for the nth term of an increasing linear sequence
T	p 112 **D** Decreasing linear sequences	Finding and using an expression for the nth term of a decreasing linear sequence

---

Essential

Sheet 264

Practice booklet pages 45 to 47

Ⓐ **Continuing sequences** (p 107)

> Sheet 264

One way to introduce the topic is described below.

◊ Explain that a sequence of numbers can be generated using a rule to go from one term to the next and that the same rule can generate different sequences. For example, adding 3 to the previous term can generate: 1, 4, 7, 10, … or 0.5, 3.5, 6.5, … and so on.

You could discuss how to use the 'constant' facility on a calculator to generate sequences.

◊ Demonstrate a variety of rules for going from one term to the next. You could display some sequences and ask pupils which rule you used to go from one term to the next. For example:

- 40, 38, 36, 34, 32, … (subtract 2 from the previous term)
- 7, 14, 28, 56, 112, … (multiply the previous term by 2)
- 1, 4, 13, 40, 121, … (multiply the previous term by 3 and add 1)
- 2, 5, 7, 12, 19, … (add the previous two terms)

Pupils may suggest alternative valid descriptions of these rules.

◊ Ask pupils to look at the sequences at the top of page 107 and, for each sequence, to find at least two different rules that could be used to generate the terms shown. What would the next three terms of each sequence be for each rule? For example:

- 1, 2, 4, 8, 16, 32, … (multiply by 2)
- 1, 2, 4, 7, 11, 16, … (add 1, add 2, add 3, …)
- 1, 2, 4, 5, 7, 8, … (add 1, add 2, add 1, add 2, …)

and

- 2, 4, 6, 8, 10, 12, … (add 2)
- 2, 4, 6, 10, 16, 26, … (add the previous two terms)

◊ Point out that, usually in work on sequences, enough terms are given so that the rule is 'obvious' and, unless stated otherwise, they should assume the most 'obvious' rule has been used.

◊ Define differences and explain that a linear sequence is one where the differences are constant. You could point out that a linear sequence is so called because graphing the terms will produce points that lie on a straight line.

B Sequences from rules (p 108)

◊ For many pupils, it will be appropriate to start with some simple linear sequences, for example $5n$ and $n + 1$ before moving on to more complex linear and non-linear sequences. Pupils may find the following kind of diagram useful:

Term numbers (n)	1	2	3	4	5	…
× 2 ↓	↓	↓	↓	↓	↓	
($2n$)	2	4	6	8	10	
+ 9 ↓	↓	↓	↓	↓	↓	
Terms of the sequence ($2n + 9$)	11	13	15	17	19	…

Pupils can then work out the first few terms for a variety of expressions, for example: $3n - 1$, $20 - n$, n^2, $\frac{6}{n}$ and investigate which give linear sequences.

◊ Emphasise that, if you know the rule for the nth term, working out other terms in the sequence is straightforward. For example, to find the 100th term for the sequence at the beginning of the section, substitute 100 into $2n + 9$ to give $(2 \times 100) + 9 = 209$ for the 100th term.

ℂ **Increasing linear sequences** (p 110)

◊ The objective of the initial discussion is to arrive at a method to find the nth term of an increasing linear sequence. The approach outlined below should help pupils see that the constant difference for a linear sequence gives the coefficient of n. With a constant difference d, the sequence dn can be compared with the original sequence to find what needs to be added or subtracted. This is the method used on page 110.

One way to introduce this method is described below.

◊ Pupils start with 1, 2, 3, 4, 5, ... and produce the sequence for $2n$ by multiplying by 2. Ask them what the differences are for this sequence and how they could have predicted this – they may have already begun to think about this in question B5 in the previous section. Now ask them to choose a number to add to or subtract from $2n$ to produce a new sequence – what are the differences for their new sequences?

They may find the following kind of diagram useful.

n	1	2	3	4	5	...	
× 2 ↓	↓	↓	↓	↓	↓		2 times table –
$2n$	2	4	6	8	10	...	the difference is 2 each time
+ 3 ↓	↓	↓	↓	↓	↓		the difference is
$2n + 3$	5	7	9	11	13	...	still 2 each time

They should find that, whatever you add or subtract, the differences remain 2, 2, 2, 2, ... each time. Ask them to try and explain this.

They can now repeat this with different initial multipliers before or after looking at the method on page 110.

◊ This work links directly with earlier work on gradient and y-intercept of straight-line graphs. Discuss the link with the constant difference of a linear sequence and the gradient of a straight-line graph. Pupils may find it helpful to draw a graph of the terms of the sequence against the term number n.

$\mathbb{D}$ **Decreasing linear sequences** (p 112)

◊ Decreasing sequences can be approached in the same way as increasing linear sequences (described in the notes for section C). For example:

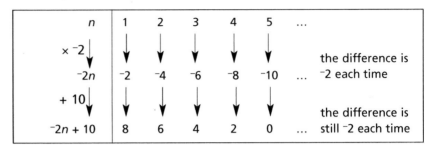

◊ You may need to discuss why $^-2n + 52$ is equivalent to $52 - 2n$.

◊ Again, this work links directly with earlier work on gradient and y-intercept of straight-line graphs.

$\mathbb{A}$ **Continuing sequences** (p 107)

A1 (a) The pupil's description: a rule is to add 4 each time.

(b) 35

A2 (a) The pupil's description, for example: the differences increase by 1 each time, giving '+ 1', '+ 2', '+ 3', '+ 4',...

(b) 26

A3

	Rule	8th term
(a)	Add 5	44
(b)	Subtract 2	14
(c)	Multiply by 2	384
(d)	Add 1.5	11.5
(e)	Multiply by 3	2187
(f)	Add 5	40

A4 Sequences A, E and F are linear.

A5 Sequence search

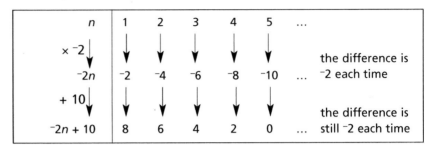

A6 (a) 2, 9, 16, **23**, 30, **37**

(b) 4, 6, **8**, **10**, 12, **14**

(c) 10, **15**, **20**, 25, 30

(d) **5**, 8, **11**, **14**, 17, **20**

*A7 Puzzle 1: the 5th term is 27
Puzzle 2: the 9th term is 24
Puzzle 3: the 6th term is 17
Puzzle 4: the 8th term is 28

B Sequences from rules (p 108)

B1 (a) The first six terms are
6, 7, 8, 9, 10, 11

(b) The differences are 1, 1, 1, 1, 1, ...
It is a linear sequence.

B2 (a) The first six terms are
1, 4, 7, 10, 13, 16

(b) The differences are 3, 3, 3, 3, 3, ...
It is a linear sequence.

B3 **Expression A ($3n$)**

(a) 3, 6, 9, 12, 15, 18

(b) Yes   (c) 300

Expression B ($2n + 5$)

(a) 7, 9, 11, 13, 15, 17

(b) Yes   (c) 205

Expression C ($5n + 2$)

(a) 7, 12, 17, 22, 27, 32

(b) Yes   (c) 502

Expression D ($3n - 1$)

(a) 2, 5, 8, 11, 14, 17

(b) Yes   (c) 299

Expression E ($150 - n$)

(a) 149, 148, 147, 146, 145, 144

(b) Yes   (c) 50

Expression F ($n^2 - 1$)

(a) 0, 3, 8, 15, 24, 35

(b) No   (c) 9999

Expression G ($^-2n + 200$)

(a) 198, 196, 194, 192, 190, 188

(b) Yes   (c) 0

B4 (a) All the expressions begin 'n ...'

(b) A: 3, 4, 5, 6, 7, 8
B: 4, 5, 6, 7, 8, 9
C: 0, 1, 2, 3, 4, 5
D: 7, 8, 9, 10, 11, 12
E: 11, 12, 13, 14, 15, 16
All the sequences are linear.

(c) They go up in 1s.

B5 (a) All the expressions begin '$2n$ ...'

(b) A: 2, 4, 6, 8, 10, 12
B: 5, 7, 9, 11, 13, 15
C: 1, 3, 5, 7, 9, 11
D: 0, 2, 4, 6, 8, 10
E: 11, 13, 15, 17, 19, 21
All the sequences are linear.

(c) They go up in 2s.

B6 (a) $4n + 1$ (b) $n + 4$ (c) $5n - 1$

(d) $3n + 7$ (e) $3n + 1$

B7 (a) C (5, 4, 3, 2, 1, ...)

(b) B (18, 16, 14, 12, 10, ...)

C Increasing linear sequences (p 110)

C1

	nth term	50th term
(a)	$3n + 6$	156
(b)	$5n - 4$	246
(c)	$2n + 5$	105
(d)	$6n - 5$	295
(e)	$n + 9$	59
(f)	$4n - 3$	197

C2 (a) The pupils' explanations, possibly:
'He has noticed that the rule to go
from one term to the next is '+ 2'.
But '$n + 2$' is not the nth term as, for
example, $5 + 2 = 7$ is not the 5th
term.'

(b) $2n + 6$

C3 (a) (4, 3) (b) (7, 3)

(c) (i) (13, 3) (ii) (31, 3)

(d) Dolphin coordinates table

Dolphin (n)	x	y
1	4	3
2	7	3
3	10	3
4	13	3
5	16	3
6	19	3
7	22	3
8	25	3
9	28	3
10	31	3

(e) $(3n + 1, 3)$ (f) (91, 3)

*C4 (a) (1, 1), (3, 2), (5, 3), (7, 4), (9, 5), ...

(b) Tabulated coordinates

(c) $(2n - 1, n)$ (d) (199, 100)

(e) $(2n - 2, n + 2)$

D Decreasing linear sequences (p 112)

D1 nth term 20th term

(a) $100 - 2n$ 60

(b) $73 - 3n$ 13

(c) $50 - n$ 30

(d) $100 - 5n$ 0

(e) $90 - 4n$ 10

(f) $50 - 3n$ $^-10$

D2 (a) (1, 11) (b) (1, 7)

(c) (i) (1, 5) (ii) (1, 1)

(d) Shark nose coordinates table

Shark (n)	x	y
1	1	11
2	1	9
3	1	7
4	1	5
5	1	3
6	1	1
7	1	$^-1$
8	1	$^-3$
9	1	$^-5$
10	1	$^-7$

(e) $(1, 13 - 2n)$

(f) Shark tail tip coordinates table

Shark (n)	x	y
1	7	10
2	7	8
3	7	6
4	7	4
5	7	2
6	7	0
7	7	$^-2$
8	7	$^-4$
9	7	$^-6$
10	7	$^-8$

(g) $(7, 12 - 2n)$ (h) (7, $^-28$)

*D3 (a) Tabulated coordinates

(b) $(3n - 2, 10 - n)$ (c) (148, $^-40$)

What progress have you made? (p 114)

1 Sequence A

(a) A rule is to add 1 (b) 15

Sequence B

(a) A rule is to subtract 1 from the first term and then continue to subtract whole numbers in order, giving '$- 1$', '$- 2$', '$- 3$', '$- 4$', ...

(b) 15

Sequence C

(a) A rule is to multiply by 2.

(b) 2048

Sequence D

(a) A rule is to subtract 2.

(b) 22

2 (a) Sequence A (6, 7, 8, 9, 10, …)

(b) Sequence D (40, 38, 36, 34, 32, …)

3 (a) 3, 8, 13, 18, 23, 28 (b) 98

4 (a) 27, 26, 25, 24 (b) 18

5 (a) $6n + 5$; 155 (b) $4n - 2$; 98

6 (a) $40 - n$; 10 (b) $154 - 4n$; 34

Practice booklet

Section A (p 45)

1 (a) Add 5   (b) 49

2   nth term   10th term
  (a) $+3$ 31
  (b) -1 11
  (c) $+2\frac{1}{2}$ $24\frac{1}{2}$
  (d) $\times 3$ 59 049

3 B, C and D are linear

4 (a) 3, 9, **15**, 21, **27**, **33**
  (b) 5, **10**, **15**, 20, 25, **30**
  (c) 4, **10**, **16**, 22, 28
  (d) **3**, 5, **7**, 9, 11, **13**

Section B (p 45)

1 **A:** (a) 5, 10, 15, 20, 25, 30
       (b) Linear   (c) 500
  B: (a) 8, 11, 14, 17, 20, 23
       (b) Linear   (c) 305
  C: (a) 1, 5, 9, 13, 17, 21
       (b) Linear   (c) 397
  D: (a) 4, 7, 12, 19, 28, 39
       (b) Not linear   (c) 10 003
  E: (a) 198, 196, 194, 192, 190, 188
       (b) Linear   (c) 0

2 (a) $n+7$ (b) $2n-1$ (c) $3n+4$
  (d) $6n-1$ (e) $4n+3$

3 (a) $12-n$ (b) $^-n+8$
  (c) $2n-4$ (d) $^-5n+3$

Section C (p 46)

1   nth term   30th term
  (a) $4n+2$ 122
  (b) $3n+7$ 97
  (c) $6n-4$ 176
  (d) $n+7$ 37
  (e) $7n-6$ 204

2 (a) (2, 2)
  (b) (i) (11, 2)   (ii) (29, 2)
  (c)

Fish (n)	x	y
1	2	2
2	5	2
3	8	2
4	11	2
5	14	2
6	17	2
7	20	2
8	23	2
9	26	2
10	29	2

  (d) $(3n-1, 2)$ (e) (74, 2)

Section D (p 47)

1   nth term   25th term
  (a) $96-3n$ 21
  (b) $162-5n$ 37
  (c) $70-n$ 45
  (d) $85-3n$ 10
  (e) $45-2n$ $^-5$

2 (a) (3, 17)   (b) (3, 1)
  (c)

Fish (n)	x	y
1	3	17
2	3	13
3	3	9
4	3	5
5	3	1
6	3	$^-3$
7	3	$^-7$
8	3	$^-11$
9	3	$^-15$
10	3	$^-19$

  (d) $(3, 21-4n)$ (e) $(3, ^-79)$

⑰ Decimals

This work lends itself to being done in manageable chunks rather than all in one go. As well as revising mental and written methods and taking them further, it includes several other topics that make use of decimals. These are listed below at the beginning of the notes to each section; revision of them could well be the basis of effective lesson starters. Checking that answers make sense is an important aspect of this work.

The work informally prepares for the idea that multiplying and dividing by powers of ten involves adding and subtracting the indices of the powers involved.

Practice booklet pages 48 to 50

Ⓐ Adding and subtracting decimals – revision (p 115)

Topics included are: range, metric units. The section also gives opportunities for backwards checking (for example A6, A9 and A10).

Ⓑ Multiplying (p 117)

Area of a rectangle is included.

An interesting enhancement to the lattice method is as follows. Keep the decimal points in the given numbers as you write them above and to the right of the lattice. Imagine these decimal points moving, respectively, 'south' and 'west' until they meet, and then going 'south west' until they reach the answer. Where they do so is the position of the decimal point in the answer. You (or the pupils) might like to work out why this works.

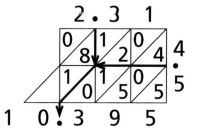

The panel at the end of the section is intended to stimulate discussion of whether it's always true that multiplying makes the number you started with bigger. The preceding work should have provided evidence that it is not true when the number you multiplied by is between 0 and 1. It may also emerge that if you start with a negative number and multiply by a number greater than 1, the result is smaller (more negative).

C **Dividing** (p 120)

Again, the section should provide evidence that dividing by a number between 0 and 1 makes the number you started with bigger.

D **Mixed questions** (p 122)

Topics included are: perimeter, area, ratio, decimal equivalents of simple fractions, rounding appropriate to a context, the effect of enlargement on a perimeter and probability ideas, including relative frequency as an estimate of probability.

E **Recurring decimals** (p 124)

The hardest part is adjusting the ruler edge to the correct place on vertical scale while also keeping it on the red dot. Pupils must check by dividing when more than one black dot seems to be a candidate, though in some cases this is because the fractions are equivalent.

A **Adding and subtracting decimals – revision** (p 115)

A1 (a) 19.1   (b) 10.2   (c) 5.32
  (d) 12.32   (e) 3.72   (f) 68.24
  (g) 41.9   (h) 24.26

A2 (a) £18.50   (b) £19.22   (c) £7.05
  (d) £5.73   (e) £12.92

A3 (a) 6.48 kg   (b) 0.68 kg

A4 0.27 m

A5 (a)   1.6
     + 1.52
     3.12

  (b)   3.8
     26.26
     30.06

  (c)   5.43
     − 2.61
     2.82

  (d)   3.61
     − 1.13
     2.48

A6 (a) 133.45   (b) 258.38   (c) 59.703
  (d) 287.7   (e) 24.198   (f) 227.395
  (g) 319.183

A7 The 3 key

A8 18.29 m

A9 1.67 m (or 167 cm)

A10 1015 ml or 1.015 litres

A11 4.372 m

A12 (a) 38 g (or 0.038 kg)

(b) 105 g

B Multiplying (p 117)

B1 (a) 6   (b) 6.3   (c) 5.4

(d) 6.4   (e) 0.06   (f) 0.24

(g) 0.6   (h) 9.9   (i) 14.56

(j) 12.6

B2 The multiplications can be in either order.

(a) **0.6 × 4** = 2.4

(b) **0.03 × 5** = 0.15

(c) **0.06 × 8** = 0.48

(d) **0.25 × 8** = 2

(e) **0.06 × 5** = 0.3

(f) **0.6 × 5** = 3

B3 (a) 85.5   (b) 31.92   (c) 61.68

(d) 723.6   (e) 399.6   (f) 594

(g) 86.88   (h) 328.07

B4 (a) £318.50   (b) £316.25   (c) £781.95

(d) £858.80   (e) £922.50

B5 (a) $\frac{1}{10} \times \frac{7}{10} = \frac{7}{100} = 0.07$

(b) $\frac{3}{10} \times \frac{1}{10} = \frac{3}{100} = 0.03$

(c) $\frac{9}{10} \times \frac{3}{10} = \frac{27}{100} = 0.27$

(d) $\frac{4}{10} \times \frac{3}{10} = \frac{12}{100} = 0.12$

(e) $\frac{8}{10} \times \frac{6}{10} = \frac{48}{100} = 0.48$

(f) $\frac{3}{10} \times \frac{5}{100} = \frac{15}{1000} = 0.015$

(g) $\frac{1}{100} \times \frac{8}{10} = \frac{8}{1000} = 0.008$

(h) $\frac{7}{10} \times \frac{7}{100} = \frac{49}{1000} = 0.049$

(i) $\frac{6}{100} \times \frac{4}{100} = \frac{24}{10000} = 0.0024$

(j) $\frac{3}{10} \times \frac{5}{10} \times \frac{7}{10} = \frac{105}{1000} = 0.105$

B6 (a) 0.9   (b) 0.3   (c) 0.08

B7 (a) 0.006   (b) 0.06   (c) 0.1

B8 (a) 0.36   (b) 0.25   (c) 0.01

(d) 0.64   (e) 0.008   (f) 0.729

(g) 0.001   (h) 0.343   (i) 0.0009

(j) 0.000 008

B9 (a) 0.9   (b) 0.4   (c) 0.07

(d) 0.3   (e) 0.6

B10 (a) False   (b) True

(c) True   (d) False

B11 (a) 238   (b) 302 000   (c) 8.22

(d) 0.826   (e) 0.0407   (f) 647 000

(g) 0.007 52   (h) 0.0588   (i) 0.002 16

(j) 41.8   (k) 9 050 000   (l) 0.003 09

B12 (a) 4.82 kg   (b) 0.15 kg   (c) 0.0103 kg

B13 (a) 120 cm   (b) 15.4 cm   (c) 7.8 cm

B14 (a) 4200 m   (b) 52 m   (c) 0.092 m

B15 (a) 2.08   (b) 0.444   (c) 0.0201

(d) 0.0246   (e) 0.064 26   (f) 6.63

(g) 1.974   (h) 9.72   (i) 0.051

(j) 13.464

B16 (a) 1.12 m^2 (b) 2.53 m^2

B17 (a) 1.026   (b) 0.010 26   (c) 0.1026

(d) 10.26   (e) 0.001 026

B18 (a) 7.222   (b) 7.222   (c) 0.7222

(d) 0.7222   (e) 0.007 222

B19 (a) 1.44   (b) 4.84   (c) 102.01

(d) 1030.301   (e) 0.512

B20 (a) True   (b) False   (c) False

(d) True   (e) True   (f) True

C Dividing (p 120)

C1 (a) 0.3   (b) 0.66   (c) 1.12

(d) 2.3   (e) 0.013

C2 (a) 20   (b) 20   (c) 20

(d) 6000   (e) 3

C3 (a) 220   (b) 6   (c) 400

(d) 900   (e) 8000

C4 (a) 960   (b) 73.5   (c) 60

(d) 17   (e) 124

C5 (a) 126.7   (b) 20.3   (c) 19.6

    (d) 54.5   (e) 2.7

C6 (a) 38.33   (b) 82.22   (c) 7.23

    (d) 0.83   (e) 1.31

C7 (a) 122   (b) 32

$\mathbb{D}$ Mixed questions (p 122)

D1 210.8 km

D2

A
$$\begin{array}{r} 24.5 \\ +\ 6.8 \\ \hline 31.3 \end{array}$$

D
$$\begin{array}{r} 13.32 \\ +\ 2.8 \\ \hline 16.12 \end{array}$$

G
$$9\,\overline{)\,13.05}\ \ 1.45$$

H
$$\begin{array}{r} 1.43 \\ \times\ 0.205 \\ \hline 28600 \\ 715 \\ \hline 0.29315 \end{array}$$

D3 (a) 22.4 cm   (b) 24.0 cm   (c) 110.8 cm

    (d) 92.8 cm   (e) 537.6 cm^2 (f) 226.8 cm^2

D4 32.854 m

D5 (a) 9.9 litres

    (b) 1.6 litres of red and 4.4 litres of white

D6 (a) 31 cm (or 31.3 cm)

    (b) 2.6 kg (or 2.59 kg)

    (c) 387 litres

    (d) 113 m (or 112.5 m)

    (e) 3.6 km

    (f) 3.8 litres (or 3.85 litres)

D7 9 trips (not 7)

D8 (a) 34.4 cm   (b) 103.2 cm

D9 (a)

Colour	Probability as a fraction	Probability as a decimal (to 2 d.p.)
Blue	$\frac{2}{7}$	0.29
Red	$\frac{4}{7}$	0.57
Yellow	$\frac{1}{7}$	0.14

    (b) Relative frequency of red = 0.68
        Relative frequency of yellow = 0.08

    (c) The relative frequency of red is higher than you would expect if the spinner is fair.

        The relative frequency of yellow is lower than you would expect if the spinner is fair.

        In spite of these differences the experiment does not prove that the spinner is not fair. There have not been enough trials to say that the relative frequencies are good estimates of the probabilities.

D10 13 × 0.4, 13 × 0.8, 13 ÷ 0.8, 13 ÷ 0.4

D11 (a) 1000   (b) 8   (c) 60

D12 £8.13

$\mathbb{E}$ Recurring decimals (p 124)

E1 (a) $\frac{1}{6}$ or $\frac{2}{12}$ (b) $\frac{4}{9}$ (c) $\frac{7}{11}$

    (d) $\frac{7}{12}$ (e) $\frac{8}{13}$ (f) $\frac{3}{7}$

E2 (a) $\frac{2}{3}$ (or $\frac{4}{6}$ etc.)   (b) $\frac{5}{6}$ or $\frac{10}{12}$

    (c) $\frac{11}{12}$ (d) $\frac{10}{11}$

    (e) $\frac{6}{7}$ (f) $\frac{4}{13}$

What progress have you made? (p 126)

1 (a) 19.1   (b) 40.9   (c) 7.2

2 (a) 1.21 (b) 3.72 (c) 4   (d) 2.8

3 (a) 85   (b) 0.501   (c) 0.744

    (d) 74   (e) 84.35   (f) 2200

4 (a) £0.76   (b) £1.14

    (c) £2.43   (d) £6.56

5 (a) 3.9 litres

    (b) 7.5 litres of yellow and 4.5 litres of blue

6 8 files (not 7)

Practice booklet

Section A (p 48)

1 (a) 13.3   (b) 7.6   (c) 4.15
   (d) 13.55   (e) 6.5   (f) 3.35

2 (a) $2.61 + 2.6 = 5.21\,$kg
   (b) $2.16 - 2.06 = 0.1\,$kg
   (c) $2.61 - 2.06 = 0.55\,$kg
   (d) 9.43 kg

3 (a) 55.91 seconds (b) 1.15 seconds

Section B (p 48)

1 E: 12   F: 1.8   R: 16.8   S: 16.12
   C: 17.12 N: 22.62 P: 22.05   T: 23.8
   A: 0.24   E: 0.1   M: 0.23   O: 0.018
   FACTOR

2 P: 0.5   R: 0.000 027 T: 0.001 U: 0.81
   A: 4.8   C: 0.2   E: 0.02   I: 4
   L: 4.464 O: 4.48   Q: 14.76 S: 4.41
   SQUARE

3 (a)

×	0.1	0.15	0.04
4	0.4	0.6	0.16
0.2	0.02	0.03	0.008
0.5	0.05	0.075	0.02

   (b)

×	0.2	0.3	0.01
5	1	1.5	0.05
0.4	0.08	0.12	0.004
7	1.4	2.1	0.07

4 (a) 0.7 m   (b) 0.26 m   (c) 0.075 m
   (d) 4.09 m   (e) 650 m

5 (a) 0.45 kg   (b) 2.8 kg
   (c) 0.038 kg   (d) 2.075 kg

Section C (p 49)

1 A: 1.75   D: 0.3   I: 0.03   P: 1.7
   E: 30   O: 0.7   R: 45   W: 7
   F: 13.1   M: 23   T: 450   U: 230
   C: 2.1   H: 12   N: 17   X: 8
   FRACTION

2 (a) 10.5   (b) 34.1   (c) 8.6

3 (a) 15   (b) 11.25 m/s

Section D (p 50)

1 9.675

2 (a) 2 m 30 cm   (b) 2.048 m
   (c) 0.252 m or 25.2 cm or 252 mm

3 (a) $3 \times 0.4 + 0.1 = 1.3$
   (b) $0.4 + 3 \times 0.2 = 1$
   (c) $(1.75 + 0.35) \times 0.1 = 0.21$
   (d) $3.2 \div 4 + 0.2 = 1$
   (e) $0.5 - 0.7 \times 0.7 = 0.01$
   (f) $0.9 \times (4.3 - 3.6) = 0.63$

4 (a) 0.85 g   (b) 14.788 g

5 (a) $0.168\,\text{m}^3$ (b) $2.44\,\text{m}^2$ (c) 12

6 (a) 60.8 kg   (b) 12.8 stones

⑱ Area of a circle

Practice booklet pages 51 and 52

Ⓐ The formula for the area of a circle (p 127)

◊ Diagrams A and B show that the area of a circle is between $2r^2$ and $4r^2$.
The data for the four given circles show that the area is about $3.14r^2$.
Pupils could confirm this for a circle of their own drawn on squared paper.

◊ The diagrams showing a circle cut into sectors and the sectors rearranged should lead to discussion of questions such as
   • Roughly what shape is the second diagram?
   • Why is it only roughly this shape?
   • What is its area, roughly?
   • What would happen if the circle were cut into more (thinner) sectors?
   • What happens as the number of sectors gets larger and larger?

Ⓑ Area and circumference (p 129)

The purpose of this section is to help pupils use the right formula – area or circumference.

Ⓒ Calculating radius given area (p 130)

◊ You may need to remind pupils about the meaning of square root.

Ⓓ Designs (p 131)

Some of these offer a logical challenge.

Ⓐ The formula for the area of a circle (p 127)

A1 (a) $113.1 \, \text{cm}^2$ (b) $176.7 \, \text{cm}^2$
   (c) $18.1 \, \text{cm}^2$ (d) $98.5 \, \text{cm}^2$
   (e) $2.5 \, \text{cm}^2$

A2 (a) $1.4 \, \text{cm}$ (b) $6.2 \, \text{cm}^2$

A3 (a) $60.8 \, \text{cm}^2$ (b) $45.4 \, \text{cm}^2$
   (c) $227.0 \, \text{cm}^2$ (d) $22.9 \, \text{cm}^2$
   (e) $63.6 \, \text{cm}^2$ (f) $22.1 \, \text{cm}^2$

A4 (a) $8.0 \, \text{cm}^2$ (b) $4.5 \, \text{cm}^2$ (c) $3.5 \, \text{cm}^2$

A5 (a) The pupil's decision
   (b) The area of the ring ($8.1 \, \text{cm}^2$) is greater than the area of the green circle ($7.1 \, \text{cm}^2$).

A6 $63.6 \, \text{m}^2$

A7 (a) $346 \, \text{cm}^2$ (b) $277 \, \text{cm}^2$

A8 The pupil's estimate. Triangle $12.5 \, \text{cm}^2$
   Circle $12.6 \, \text{cm}^2$ Rectangle $13 \, \text{cm}^2$

A9 The two 10 cm diameter pizzas have combined area (157.1 cm^2) of half that of the 20 cm diameter pizza (314.2 cm^2) but cost $\frac{5}{6}$ of the price.

The 20 cm diameter pizza is better value.

𝔹 Area and circumference (p 129)

B1 (a) (i) 13.8 cm   (ii) 15.2 cm^2

(b) (i) 10.1 cm   (ii) 8.0 cm^2

(c) (i) 32.0 cm   (ii) 81.7 cm^2

(d) (i) 27.0 cm   (ii) 58.1 cm^2

(e) (i) 101.8 cm   (ii) 824.5 cm^2

B2 (a) 141.0 cm^2 (b) 60.9 cm
(c) 463.8 cm^2

B3 (a) $40\pi = 125.7$ m   (b) 6513.3 m^2

B4 (a) 11.6 cm^2 (b) 21.5%

B5 264.2 cm^2

B6 (a) 1520 mm^2 (b) 800 mm^2
(c) 8170 mm^2 (d) 5810 mm^2
(e) 82 450 mm^2
The numbers have been multiplied by 100, indicating 1 cm^2 = 100 mm^2

ℂ Calculating radius given area (p 130)

C1 1.95 cm

C2 (a) 2.52 cm   (b) 4.0 cm   (c) 6.2 cm
(d) 1.0 cm   (e) 0.5 cm   (f) 0.7 cm

C3 (a) 3.337 790 589...   (b) 21.0 cm
(c) If $r = 3.3$, circumference $= 20.7$ cm

C4 23.4 cm

C5

Radius	Diameter	Circumference	Area
12.8 cm	25.6 cm	80.4 cm	514.7 cm^2
27.9 cm	55.8 cm	175.3 cm	2445.4 cm^2
11.6 cm	23.1 cm	72.6 cm	419.4 cm^2
4.5 cm	9.0 cm	28.4 cm	64.2 cm^2

𝔻 Designs (p 131)

D1 (a) 3.4 cm^2 (b) 3.4 cm^2 (c) 2.3 cm^2

D2 (a) 6.3 cm^2 (b) 9.4 cm^2

D3 53.7 cm^2

What progress have you made? (p 131)

1 (a) (i) 78.5 cm^2 (ii) 31.4 cm

(b) (i) 9.1 m^2 (ii) 10.7 m

(c) (i) 8494.9 cm^2 (ii) 326.7 cm

2 104.9 cm^2

Practice booklet

Section A (p 51)

1 (a) 141 cm^2 (b) 61 cm^2 (c) 196 cm^2

2 (a) 221.6... cm^2 (b) 98.5... cm^2
(c) 123.2 cm^2 to 1 d.p.

3 197.9 m^2

4 (a) 121 cm^2 (b) 57 cm^2

Section B (p 51)

1 (a) 13.2 cm   (b) 91.6 cm^2
(c) 55.3 cm   (d) 122.7 cm^2

Section C (p 52)

1 $r = \sqrt{\dfrac{A}{\pi}} = \sqrt{\dfrac{30}{\pi}} = 3.1$ cm

2 (a) 3.8 cm   (b) 5.2 cm   (c) 1.4 cm
(d) 3.3 cm   (e) 6.4 cm   (f) 2.4 cm

3 (a) 7.4 cm   (b) 23.3 cm

Section D (p 52)

1 (a) (i) 25.7 cm   (ii) 39.3 cm^2

(b) (i) 44.8 cm   (ii) 98.5 cm^2

(c) (i) 82.3 cm   (ii) 201.7 cm^2

(d) (i) 56.5 cm   (ii) 62.8 cm^2

Review 3 (p 132)

1 8.56

2 3210 metres

3 4, 9, 14, 19, 24

4 150°

5 The years do not go up steadily so a decline in the rate of increase between 1996 and 2002 is concealed.

6 0.04 and 5

7 (a) $4n - 2$ (b) 78

8 (a) 1.55   (b) 3.19   (c) 0.54

9 (a) 72°   (b) 108°

10 (a) F   (b) F   (c) T   (d) F

11 110.39

12 Volume is 20.28 cm^3
   Surface area is 54.34 cm^2

13 (a)
```
7 | 1 4
6 | 0 0 1 2 3 3 5 8 9 9
5 | 1 1 3 4 6 8 9 9
4 | 0 1 2 5 7 8
3 | 1 6 9
2 | 2 8
1 | 0 0 1 3 4 4 5
0 | 5 6 6 8
```

   (b) There are mostly older people, but there are also some children and users in their early teens.
   There are not many in their late teens or their late teens or their twenties or thirties.
   Hypotheses about the under-represented age groups might include the following.
   They have less time for reading.
   There are other things that require their time on a Saturday afternoon.
   They can afford to buy books so do not use a library much.

   (c) 47.5; it is of little use when the sample has two 'humps' like this.

14 (a) 30   (b) 9   (c) 3.4   (d) 6.5

15 $\frac{1}{4} = 0.25$ $\frac{2}{3} = 0.66\,666\ldots$
   $\frac{5}{100} = 0.05$ $\frac{2}{9} = 0.22\,222\ldots$
   $\frac{4}{5} = 0.8$

16 12

17 $40 - 3n$

18 (a) A: 1.20, B: 1.33, C: 1.49, D: 1.49, E: 1.41
   (b) Frames C and D

19 (a) Table completed with 28.27 and 50.27
   (b) 3.14, 6.29, 9.42, 12.57
   (c) The ratios are not the same so A is not directly proportional to r.

20 (a)
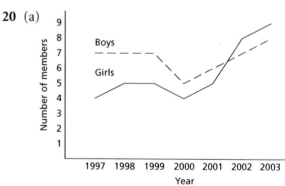

   (b) To start with there were more boys than girls. Then the number of girls increased slightly while the number of boys remained steady.
   During 2000 there was a general drop in numbers.
   After that, membership increased steadily, but the girls' rate of increase was greater than the boys', so by the end of 2003 there were slightly more girls than boys.

   (c) (i) 36%   (ii) 53%

21 $8.64\,cm^2$

22 $n = 7.0$

23 (a) Mean = 2.40 cm, median = 2.6 cm
The median is greater.

  (b) 8.8 cm, 16.3 cm, 27.0 cm, 17.6 cm, 5.7 cm

  (c) Mean = 15.08 cm, median = 16.3 cm
The median is again greater.
The scale factor is 6.28, which strongly suggests 2π.

  (d) $6.2\,cm^2$, $21.2\,cm^2$, $58.1\,cm^2$, $24.6\,cm^2$, $2.5\,cm^2$

  (e) Mean = $22.52\,cm^2$, median = $21.2\,cm^2$
Now the mean is greater.

24 9.77 m

Mixed questions 3 (Practice booklet p 53)

1 (a) 3.1, 12.6, 28.3, 50.3

  (b) The ratios are not the same value

2 Perimeter = 33.42 cm
Area = $66.37\,cm^2$

3 $a = 109°$, $b = 71°$, $c = 45°$

4 (a) Ratios are all 2.5   (b) Yes

  (c) $C = 2.5W$ (d) £32.50

5 8.0 cm

6 56°

7 8 grams

8 (a) (3, 3)

  (b) Table with 3, 7, 11, 15, 19, 23 in the x-column and 3, 3, 3, 3, 3, 3 in the y-column

  (c) $(4n - 1, 3)$ (d) (199, 3)

9 112°

10 (a) $78.5\,cm^2$ (b) 5 cm

  (c) $65\,cm^2$ (d) 83%

11 27.3

12 Exterior angles are all 20°.
Interior angles are all 160°.

13 (a) T   (b) F   (c) T

14 £40.74

15 $0.3n + 0.9$

16 3770 metres or 3.77 km

17 (a) 0.768   (b) 40   (c) 0.7

  (d) 5.6

The right connections

This unit is about handling bivariate data. Pupils interpret and draw scatter diagrams, identify positive and negative correlation and draw lines of best fit on scatter graphs.

Essential

Squared paper
Stopwatches, reaction rulers made from sheet 141
Traffic cones, tape measures

Practice booklet pages 56 and 57

Ⓐ 'The Missing Link' (p 135)

This is a short introductory task to introduce scatter diagrams.
The answers are:
A Phil, B Lemon, C Howie, D Biffo, E Aaron, F Stix

Ⓑ Drawing scatter diagrams (p 136)

Squared paper

◊ You may need to explain the use of jagged lines on one or both of the axes.

B2 The 'bleep test' is a standard fitness measure used in PE. It is based on the 'shuttle run' described in section E. A score is achieved based on how many 'runs' can be achieved in a certain period. Some pupils may need support concentrating on just two out of the three columns at a time.

C Correlation and lines of best fit (p 138)

◊ Pupils are likely to ask how they judge a line of best fit. The usual rule of thumb is to ensure that there are equal numbers of points either side of the line, but there are lots of lines that obey this but in no way fit the data. Clearly, the better the correlation, the easier it is to fit a line. In fact, unless the correlation is strong it is not worth trying.

◊ The main purpose of drawing a line is to estimate other values where this makes sense. Estimating outside the range of data is hazardous.

D Quarters (p 140)

◊ This technique is the basis of a method used for quantifying correlation in a branch of statistics called 'exploratory data analysis'.

E Correlation in surveys and experiments (p 142)

Stopwatches, reaction ruler made from sheet 141, cones, tape measures

◊ The fitness tests are a good way to develop skills in using and applying mathematics. Trialling has shown the exercises on this page do not require specialised supervision. With negotiation they could be done in a PE lesson. All but step-ups are accessible to pupils in wheelchairs. There are many other activities which could be used if you have equipment or facilities, for example standing jump (chalk on wall), peak flow meters used by asthmatics, grip meters, and so on.

◊ When the data has been collected pupils will need to record the class data on a 'spreadsheet' style grid which can be photocopied and distributed.

◊ Pupils should make their own hypotheses first and then test them using the available data. Presenting a paper is a good way for pupils to report their findings.

 This activity is enhanced by using spreadsheets or graphical calculators to process the data.

B Drawing scatter diagrams (p 136)

B1

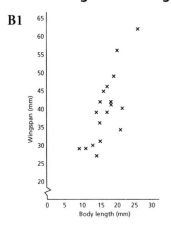

(a) Yes   (b) No   (c) Yes

B2 (a)

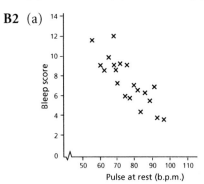

Pupils with a lower rest pulse rate generally have a higher bleep score.

(b)

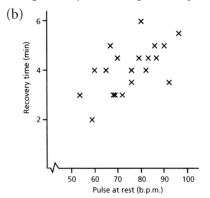

Pupils with a lower pulse at rest generally recover it more quickly.

(c)

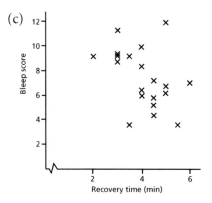

Pupils with a low recovery time generally have a higher bleep score.

C Correlation and lines of best fit (p 138)

C1 (a) Taller people tend to weigh more.

(b) Cars with bigger engines tend to go faster.

(c) People with longer legs generally run 100 m faster.

(d) Height and maths result are not linked.

C2 (a) The pupil's graph showing negative correlation

(b) The pupil's graph showing zero correlation

C3 (a) Positive   (b) Positive

(c) Negative   (d) Zero

C4 (a) 19 cm   (b) 22.8 cm   (c) 25.4 cm

C5 (a) 173 cm

(b) Not very reliable. You can see from the diagram that people with that size feet have a wide range of heights.

C6 (a)

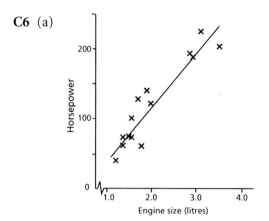

(b) The horsepower of a 2.5 litre car would be about 150.

C7 (a)

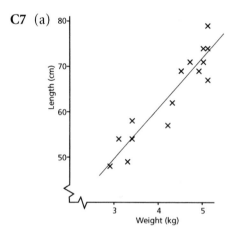

(b) (i) 60 cm (ii) 48 cm (iii) 56 cm
(iv) 80 cm

(c) 5.1 kg

(d) 7 kg; the estimate would not be reliable because it is outside the range of the data.

C8 (a)

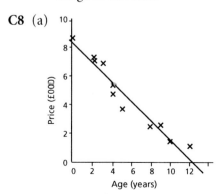

(b) About £3500 (c) About 13 years

Ⅾ **Quarters** (p 140)

D1 (a) There would be more points in downward diagonal.

(b) There would be roughly equal numbers in both diagonals.

D2

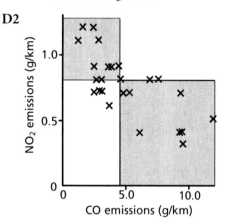

There are 4 crosses in the upward diagonal, 16 in the downward diagonal (5 on line) which suggests negative correlation.

What progress have you made? (p 143)

1

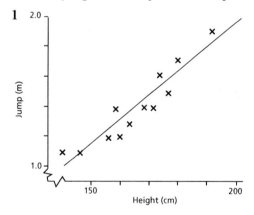

2 Taller people generally jump further.

3 (a) Positive

(b) The pupil's sketches of negative and zero correlation

4 (a) A line of best fit (see diagram above)

(b) About 1.7 m

(c) Sam: worse
Mel: better
Chris: as expected

Practice booklet

Section B (p 56)

1 (a)

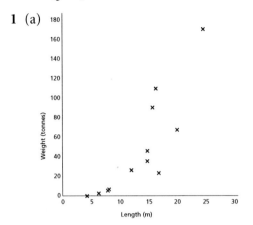

(b) Generally longer whales weigh more.

2 (a) The Sei and the Fin

(b) 26 and 20 knots respectively

(c) This suggests these two whales are slender for their lengths and are more streamlined.

Sections C and D (p 57)

1 (a) There is no correlation between weight and speed.

(b) There is no evidence to support the biologist's hypothesis.

2 (a), (b)

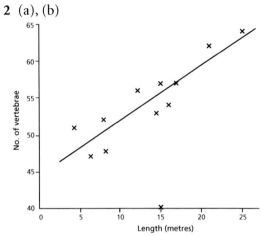

(c) Approximately 60

3 Median length = 14.8 m
Median vertebra = 53.5

Quartering gives 10 in the upward diagonal and 2 in the downward diagonal.
This suggests a positive correlation.

㉒ Algebra problems

This unit introduces equations where the unknown is subtracted from a constant. It includes problems leading to such equations, though many pupils will find such problems difficult.

p 144 **A** Take off	Revision of equations with constants subtracted
p 145 **B** Subtracted unknowns	Equations with the unknown subtracted from a constant
p 146 **C** Number puzzles	Translating number puzzles to equations
p 148 **D** Mixed problems	Problems leading to equations with subtracted unknowns

Practice booklet pages 58 to 61

Ⓐ Take off (p 144)

*A4   This question may be used as a lead-in to the next section.

Ⓑ Subtracted unknowns (p 145)

Without pupils looking at the solutions at the top of page 145, you may wish them to discuss how to solve equations involving subtracted unknowns, such as $120 - 7n = n + 16$. They can then check that their method works by substituting back into the original equation.

Discussion of the different methods pupils have employed can then be used to bring out the following:

- It does not matter what you do first to the equation, as long as you do the same thing to both sides.
- It is often better to deal with the unknowns first, and then the numbers, as this leads to fewer mistakes being made.

It may also be a good thing to discuss some of the common pitfalls that arise, such as those exemplified in question B3.

C Number puzzles (p 146)

(p 146)

◊ The introductory teacher-led section draws attention to two points:

  • Some number puzzles (like Jordan's) can be solved by working backwards and some (like Abbie's) cannot.

  • Abbie's puzzle leads to an equation with the unknown subtracted from a constant.

◊ In a number puzzle, the two sentences 'I take the result away from 12' and 'I take 12 away from the result' lead to quite different equations. This linguistic distinction will need drawing out.

C8 Pupils are unlikely to have met an equation with an infinite number of solutions. They may need discussion to be clear that Emma and Jake could have thought of any number.

D Mixed problems (p 148)

◊ These problems lead to equations with subtracted unknowns.

The section will probably prove difficult for many pupils. The SMP Interact material will cover the ground more thoroughly at key stage 4, so it may be omitted if wished.

Here n is used for the variable in solutions to number puzzles and x in problems. Pupils will probably use several different letters.

A Take off (p 144)

A1
(a) $x = 10$ (b) $x = 12$
(c) $x = 13$ (d) $x = 5$
(e) $a = 13$ (f) $t = 4$
(g) $y = 10$ (h) $u = 4$

A2 Rhys starts with 5.

A3
(a) $3n + 36$ or $36 + 3n$
(b) $5n + 8$ or $8 + 5n$
(c) $3n + 36 = 5n + 8$
    $n = 14$ (coins in a bag)

*A4 If Imran's number is n then
$120 - 7n = n + 16$.
$n = 13$; Imran thought of 13.

B Subtracted unknowns (p 145)

B1 (a) $36 + 3x = 100 - 5x$
           $36 + \mathbf{8}x = 100$ (add $5x$ to both)
                $\mathbf{8}x = 64$ (take 36 off both)
                $x = \mathbf{8}$ (divide both by 8)

(b) The pupil's check, such as:
    l.h.s. $= 36 + 3 \times 8 = 36 + 24 = 60$
    r.h.s. $= 100 - 5 \times 8 = 100 - 40 = 60$.

B2 (a) $25 - x = 40 - 4x$
           $\mathbf{25 + 3x = 40}$ (add $4x$ to both)
                $\mathbf{3x = 15}$ (take 25 off both)
                $x = \mathbf{5}$ (divide both by 3)

(b) The pupil's check

B3 (a) $25 - x = 10 + 2x$
           $25 = 10 + 3x$ (add x to both)
           $15 = 3x$ (take 10 off both)
           $5 = x$ (divide both by 3)

(b) $4n - 15 = 5 - n$
    $5n - 15 = 5$ (add n to both)
    $5n = 20$ (add 15 to both)
    $n = 4$ (divide both by 5)

(c) $11 - 2d = 35 - 4d$
    $11 + 2d = 35$ (add $4d$ to both)
        $2d = 24$ (take 11 off both)
         $d = 12$ (divide both by 2)

(d) $6j - 20 = 100 - 2j$
    $8j - 20 = 100$ (add $2j$ to both)
        $8j = 120$ (add 20 to both)
         $j = 15$ (divide both by 8)

B4 (a) $f = 11$ (b) $a = 31$
    (c) $w = 11$ (d) $e = 3$
    (e) $g = 0$ (f) $x = 15$
    (g) $h = 2\frac{1}{2}$ (h) $r = 6$
    (i) $y = 10$ (j) $h = 50$

$\mathbb{C}$ Number puzzles (p 146)

C1 (a) Puzzle 1 fits C; puzzle 2 fits B.

    (b) For puzzle 1, I thought of 2.
        For puzzle 2, I thought of 6.

C2 (a) The equation is $25 - 2n = 3n$
        I thought of 5.

    (b) The equation is $63 - 3n = n + 7$
        I thought of 14.

C3 (a) The equation is $48 - 6n = 2n$
        I thought of 6.

    (b) The equation is $67 - 4n = 83 - 6n$
        I thought of 8.

    (c) The equation is $33 - 5n = n - 3$
        I thought of 6.

    (d) The equation is $62 - 5n = 2n - 1$
        I thought of 9.

C4 The equation is $36 - 5n = 2n - 6$
    They thought of 6.

C5 The equation is $86 - 6n = 46 - 2n$
    They thought of 10.

C6 $3(4 - y) = 2y - 3$
    $12 - 3y = 2y - 3$ (multiply brackets)
        $12 = \mathbf{5y} - 3$ (add **3y** to both)
        $\mathbf{15} = 5y$ (add **3** to both)
        $\mathbf{3} = y$ (divide both by **5**)

C7 (a) $j = 6$ (b) $t = 16$
    (c) $f = 3$ (d) $h = 8$
  *(e) $d = {}^-1$ *(f) $a = {}^-2$

C8 The equation is $12 - 2n = 2(6 - n)$
leading to $12 - 2n = 12 - 2n$. Since this is
true for any value of n, it is impossible to
say which number they started with.

***C9** The equation has no solutions.

$\mathbb{D}$ Mixed problems (p 148)

***D1** The equation is $43 - 4x = 79 - 10x$
The cost of a CD is £6.

***D2** The equation is $320 - 17x = 500 - 27x$
    (a) One bow needs 18 cm of ribbon.
    (b) They each have 14 cm left.

***D3** The equation is $5x - 62 = 3x - 28$
    (a) One packet holds 17 Fruitees.
    (b) They each have 23 Fruitees left.

***D4** The equation is $789 - 27x = 657 - 21x$
    (a) One box holds 22 chocolates.
    (b) They each had 195 chocolates left.

***D5** (a)

Pattern no	1	2	3	4	5	6
No of tiles	7	13	19	25	31	37

    (b) Number of tiles $= 6n + 1$
    (c) $6n + 1 = 1327$
        Pattern number 221 has 1327 tiles.

Equation puzzles

$a = 5$ or $^-5$ $b = 6$ or $^-6$ $c = 7$ or $^-7$
$d = 8$ or $^-8$ $e = 2$ $f = 2$
$g = 16$ $h = 0.1$ $i = {}^-3$
$j = 7$ $k = 3$ $l = 4$

What progress have you made? (p 150)

1 (a) $x = 7$ (b) $x = 7$

   (c) $x = 12$ (d) $x = 10$

2 $99 - 7n = 4n$; $n = 9$

3 They both thought of 13.

Practice booklet

Section B (p 58)

1 (a) $35 - 4n = 6n - 5$
     $35 = \mathbf{10}n - 5$ (add $4n$ to both sides)
     $40 = \mathbf{10}n$ (add 5 to both sides)
      $\mathbf{4} = \mathbf{n}$ (divide both sides by 10)

   (b) The pupil's check

2 (a) $25 + 2x = 95 - 5x$
     $\mathbf{25 + 7x = 95}$ (add $5x$ to both sides)
        $\mathbf{7x = 70}$ (take 25 off both sides)
         $\mathbf{x = 10}$ (divide both sides by 7)

   (b) The pupil's check

3 $20 - 4n = 5 + n$
   $20 = 5 + 5n$ (add $4n$ to both sides)
   $15 = 5n$ (take 5 from both sides)
    $3 = n$ (divide both sides by 5)

4 (a) $g = 10$ (b) $j = 8$

   (c) $y = 12$ (d) $r = 6$

   (e) $k = 26$ (f) $h = 9$

   (g) $e = 5$ (h) $q = 13$

Section C (p 59)

1 (a) The equation is $100 - 6n = 4n$
     I thought of 10.

   (b) The equation is $56 - 4n = 92 - 7n$
     I thought of 12.

2 The equation is $6n - 24 = 40 - 2n$
   They thought of 8.

3 $4(5 - y) = 3(y + 2)$
   $20 - 4y = 3y + 6$ (multiply out brackets)
    $20 = \mathbf{7}y + 6$ (add $4y$ to both sides)
    $\mathbf{14 = 7y}$ (take **6** from both sides)
     $\mathbf{2 = y}$ (divide both sides by **7**)

4 (a) $x = 3$ (b) $a = 4$

   (c) $r = 6$ (d) $v = 7$

 *(e) $b = {}^-1$ *(f) $w = {}^-3$

Section D (p 60)

*1 (a) $95 - 15n$ (b) $107 - 17n$

   (c) The equation is $95 - 15n = 107 - 17n$;
     $n = 6$

   (d) 6 chocolate drops decorate each cake.

   (e) They each have 5 chocolate drops left.

*2 The equation is $6x - 25 = 5x - 19$

   (a) 6 cards are in a pack.

   (b) They each have 11 cards left.

*3 The equation is $4x + 5.50 = 3x + 10$

   (a) Their hourly rate is £4.50.

   (b) They each earn £23.50.

*4 (a)

Pattern no	1	2	3	4	5
No. of matchsticks	5	**9**	**13**	**17**	**21**

   (b) Number of matchsticks = $4n + 1$

   (c) $4n + 1 = 1449$; $n = 362$
     Pattern number 362 has 1449 tiles.

*5 $a = 21$ $b = 9$ or $^-9$ $c = 5$

  $d = 5$ or $^-5$ $e = 5$ or $^-5$ $f = 3$

  $g = 2$ $h = 0.5$ $j = ^-2$

Essential	Optional
Tracing paper	Transparencies with parallel lines drawn on
Practice booklet page 62	

Ⓐ **Angle relationships – revision** (p 151)

Simple angle relationships are revised, then used in finding missing angles. When pupils do more advanced angle chasing in key stage 4, they are often reluctant to write justifications for their results. So here they are asked to give explanations of simple problems orally, with the aim of building confidence. You can extend this to writing explanations, emphasising that they should be brief but clear. Pupils are often reluctant to refer to angles by the letters that label vertices. Encourage them to do so with these simple examples.

A12 You may have to remind pupils of the sets of facts that fix triangles (in 'Constructions' in the preceding book).

Ⓑ **Parallel lines and angles** (p 153)

Tracing paper

◊ This is best done as a teacher led activity, using an OHP and two sheets of acetate on which the parallel lines have been drawn. Pupils could then come out and point to angles that are the same size. Discussion can then focus on how the positions of such angles are related.

Ⓐ **Angle relationships – revision**
(p 151)

A1 360°

A2 180°

A3 180°

A4 Angles at A and C are the same.

A5 They are the same.

A6 Angles A, C and E are equal;
angles at B, D and F are equal.

A7 (a) It has rotation symmetry, order 2 with the centre of rotation where the diagonals cross. In general a parallelogram does not have reflection symmetry (though the special cases rectangle and square have).

(b) Angles at P and R are equal;
angles at Q and S are equal.

A8 (a) 72°; T (b) 126°; P (c) 60°; Q
(d) 34°; R (e) 40°; S

A9 (a) 101° (Angles ABD and DBC are angles on a straight line, so they add up to 180°.
So angle DBC = 180° − 79° = 101°.)

(b) 37° (The angles at E, F and G are angles of a triangle, so they add up to 180°. So
∠G = 180° − (58° + 85°) = 37°.)

(c) 48° (The angles HJI and LJK are vertically opposite, so they are equal.)

(d) 142° (The angles MNP, PNO and MNO are angles round a point, so they add up to 360°. So ∠MNO = 360° − (124° + 94°) = 142°)

(e) 73° (The angles at Q and R are equal because this is an isosceles triangle.)

A10 (a) 65°: ∠ACB = 180° − 120° = 60°
(angles on a straight line)
∠ABC = 180° − (55° + 60°) = 65°
(angles of a triangle)

(b) 68°: ∠IGH = 180° − (32° + 80°) = 68°
(angles of a triangle)
∠EGF = ∠IGH = 68°
(vertically opposite angles)

(c) 73°: ∠LJK = 360° − 322° = 38°
(angles round a point)
∠JKL = 180° − (38° + 69°) = 73°
(angles of a triangle)

(d) 30°: ∠OMN = ∠MON = 75°
(angles in an isosceles triangle)
∠ONM = 180° − (75° + 75°) = 30°
(angles of a triangle)

(e) 58°: ∠RQS = 180° − (72° + 50°) = 58°
(angles of a triangle)
∠TQS = 180° − (64° + 58°) = 58°
(angles on a straight line)

A11 (a) 53°
∠ABE = ∠CBD = 65°
(vertically opposite angles)
∠A = 180° − (62° + 65°) = 53°
(angles of a triangle)

(b) 46°
∠G + ∠F = 180° − 88° = 92°
(angles of a triangle)
But as they are equal (in an isosceles triangle) they each are half of 92°, which is 46°.

(c) 124°
∠KIJ = 180° − (90° + 34°) = 56°
(angles of a triangle)
∠HIJ = 180° − 56° = 124°
(angles on a straight line)

(d) 73°
∠LMP = ∠L = 73°
(isosceles triangle)
∠NMO = ∠LMP = 73°
(vertically opposite angles)

(e) 76°
∠TRU = 180° − (65° + 62°) = 53°
(angles on a straight line)
∠RUT = 180° − (53° + 51°) = 76°
(angles of a triangle)

(f) 24°
∠VWX = 360° − 282° = 78°
(angles round a point)
∠X = 78° (isosceles triangle)
∠V = 180° − (78° + 78°) = 24°
(angles of a triangle)

A12 Triangles ACB and HGI are congruent.
(∠I = 53°, so the same two angles and the same side between them have been given, thus 'fixing' the triangle.)

Ⓑ **Parallel lines and angles** (p 153)

B1 (a) *e* and *f*   (b) *d* and *e* (or *c* and *f*)
(c) *a* and *b* (or *c* and *d*)
(d) *a* and *b* (or *c* and *d*, whichever pair was not given for (c))

B2 (a) *s* and *t* (or *u* and *v*)
(b) *u* and *v* (or *s* and *t*)
(c) *s* and *u*
(d) *t* and *u* (or *s* and *v*)
(e) *s* and *v* (or *t* and *u*)

B3 (a) 53° (alternate angles)

   (b) 42° (vertically opposite angles)

   (c) 106° (corresponding angles)

   (d) 45° (alternate angles)

   (e) 79° (corresponding angles)

   (f) 130° (alternate angles)

   (g) 121° (vertically opposite angles)

   (h) 111° (corresponding angles)

B4 (a) 70° (B then A) (b) 60° (D then C)

   (c) 55° (B then F) (d) 51° (G then C)

What progress have you made? (p 155)

1 (a) 127°   (b) 82°   (c) 136°

   (d) 71°   (e) 152°

2 (a) ? = 360° − (123° + 110°) = 127
      (angles round a point add up to 360°)

   (b) ? = 180° − (38° + 60°) = 82°
       (angles of a triangle add up to 180°)

   (c) ? = 180° − 44° = 136°
       (angles on a straight line add up to 180°)

   (d) ? = 71° (the two angles marked are corresponding angles)

   (e) The third angle of the triangle is
       180° − (80° + 72°) = 28°
       (angles of a triangle add up to 180°)
       ? = 180° − 28° = 152° (angles on a straight line add up to 180°)

Practice booklet

Section A (p 62)

1 (a) 120°   (b) 55°   (c) 43°

   (d) 37°   (e) 38°

2 (a) 147°
      ∠CBD = 180° − (47° + 50°) = 83°
      (angles in a triangle)
      ∠ABD = 360° − (130° + 83°) = 147°
      (angles round a point)

   (b) 109°
       ∠EGF = ∠EFG = 71°
       (in an isosceles triangle)
       ∠EGH = 180° − 71° = 109°
       (angles on a straight line)

   (c) 63°
       ∠MKL = ∠IKJ = 65°
       (vertically opposite)
       ∠MLK = 180° − (52° + 65°) = 63°
       (angles in a triangle)

   (d) 65°
       ∠NOP = 360° − 310° = 50°
       (angles round a point)
       ∠ONP + ∠NPO = 180° − 50° = 130°
       (angles in a triangle)
       Since angles ONP and NPO are equal they are each half of 130°, which is 65°.

Section B (p 62)

1 (a) Corresponding angles

   (b) Vertically opposite angles

   (c) Alternate angles

2 (a) 81°: ∠ACB = ∠ECD = 81°
      (vertically opposite)
      ∠EDC = ∠ECD = 81°
      (in an isosceles triangle)

   (b) 111°: ∠GHI = 360° − 249° = 111°
       (angles round a point)
       ∠FIJ = ∠GHI = 111°
       (corresponding angles)

   (c) 80°: ∠NLM = 360° − 260° − 40° = 60°
       ∠LNM = ∠KLN = 40°
       (alternate angles)
       ∠LMN = 180° − 60° − 40° = 80°
       (angles of a triangle)

   (d) 62°: ∠OQR = ∠POQ = 56°
       (alternate angles)
       ∠QOR + ∠QRO = 180 − 56 = 124°
       (angles in a triangle)
       Since angles QOR and QRO are equal (in an isosceles triangle) they are each half of 124°, which is 62°.

Transformations

Essential	Optional
Sheet 246 (one per pair)	Mirrors
Cards made from sheet 247	Tracing paper
(one set per pair)	
Counters	
Sheet 265	
Practice booklet pages 63 to 67	

𝔸 Translations and vectors (p 156)

Pupils have worked with translations earlier in the course but have not used column vectors to describe them.

> Sheet 246 (one per pair)
> Cards made from sheet 247 (one set per pair)
> Counters
> Optional: tracing paper

◊ Review the ideas and vocabulary of a point or shape mapping to an image. The vectors **a** to **m** are intended to be used for teacher-led oral questions on translations and column vectors.

◊ 'Vector snakes and ladders' provides self-checking practice in relating a column vector to the 'move' it represents. It also serves to strengthen the idea that a vector can operate anywhere on the grid: it does not have fixed start and finish points.

As described in the pupils' book the game is one of pure chance, but it can be adapted to involve strategy as follows. Each player is dealt four vector cards and the rest are placed in a pile face down. On their turn players move their counter according to one of the vectors in their hand,

'This was excellent. My group got very animated and learnt the four directions with +/– quicker than any other group that I have taught.'

then put the used card at the bottom of the pack and take a new one from the top; or, *without moving their counter*, they may replace a card they hold with the unknown card from the top of the pack.

B **Reflection** (p 158)

> Sheet 265
> Optional: mirrors

C **Rotation** (p 159)

Rotations that are multiples of 90° are covered. It is intended that pupils identify centres of rotation by inspection or by using tracing paper.

> Optional: tracing paper

◊ You may wish to emphasise that, say, a rotation of 90° clockwise about a point is equivalent to a rotation of 270° anticlockwise about the same point. Answers are given using the smallest angle possible.

D **Translation, reflection and rotation** (p 161)

> Optional: tracing paper, mirrors

E **Combining transformations** (p 162)

> Optional: tracing paper, mirrors

E9 Pupils could investigate other pairs of parallel lines to find that the single transformation is always a translation of twice the distance between the lines.

Ⓐ Translations and vectors (p 156)

A1 (a) D (b) G (c) C (d) B
(e) K (f) F (g) H (h) E
(i) J (j) I

A2 (a) $\begin{bmatrix} 7 \\ 3 \end{bmatrix}$ (b) $\begin{bmatrix} 2 \\ -3 \end{bmatrix}$ (c) $\begin{bmatrix} -9 \\ -3 \end{bmatrix}$

(d) $\begin{bmatrix} 0 \\ 3 \end{bmatrix}$ (e) $\begin{bmatrix} 0 \\ -7 \end{bmatrix}$ (f) $\begin{bmatrix} -6 \\ 4 \end{bmatrix}$

A3 (a), (b), (c)

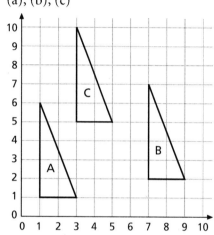

(d) $\begin{bmatrix} 4 \\ -3 \end{bmatrix}$ (e) $\begin{bmatrix} -4 \\ 3 \end{bmatrix}$

Ⓑ Reflection (p 158)

B1 (a) Kite

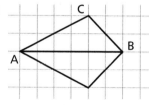

(b) Arrowhead

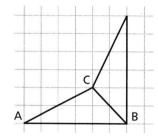

B2 (a) E and G

(b) A and B   A and F   B and E
C and H   D and E   D and G
E and F   F and G

B3 (a) (i) 4
(ii) 4
(iii) 16

(b), (c)

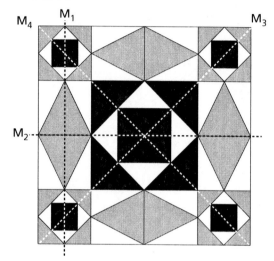

(d) (i) M_2
(ii) M_3
(iii) M_4
(iv) M_1

B4 (a), (b)

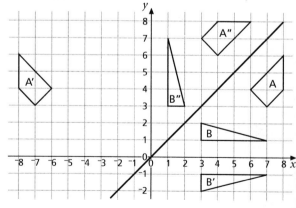

ℂ **Rotation** (p 159)

C1 (a)

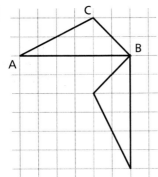

(b) Parallelogram

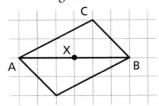

C2 (a), (b), (c)

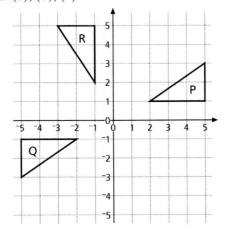

(d) A clockwise rotation of 90°
about (0, 0)

C3 (a) X   (b) Y

C4 (a) H   (b) H

C5 An anticlockwise rotation of 90° about Z

C6 (a) X   (b) Z

C7 (a) J   (b) L

C8 (a) A rotation of 180° about Z

(b) A rotation of 180° about W

(c) A clockwise rotation of 90° about Y

(d) An anticlockwise rotation of 90°
about Y

𝔻 **Translation, reflection and rotation** (p 161)

D1 (a) C   (b) K   (c) B   (d) D

D2 (a) A reflection in M_3

(b) A translation of $\begin{bmatrix} 12 \\ 0 \end{bmatrix}$

(c) A rotation of 180° about Y

(d) A clockwise rotation of 90° about Y

(e) A rotation of 180° about X

D3 (a) A translation of $\begin{bmatrix} 12 \\ 12 \end{bmatrix}$

(b) A reflection in M_3

(c) An anticlockwise rotation of 90°
about Y

(d) A rotation of 180° about Z

𝔼 **Combining transformations** (p 162)

E1 (a), (b), (c)

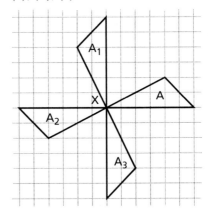

(d) Rotation of 180° about X

(e) Rotation of 90° clockwise about X

E2

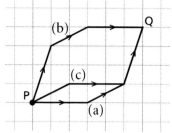

You always finish at Q, whatever order you draw the three vectors.

E3

The third vector is $\begin{bmatrix} 2 \\ -1 \end{bmatrix}$.

E4 (a) $\begin{bmatrix} 4 \\ 2 \end{bmatrix}$, $\begin{bmatrix} 2 \\ 1 \end{bmatrix}$ and $\begin{bmatrix} 3 \\ 1 \end{bmatrix}$

(b) No, you can use them in any order.

E5 (a) $\begin{bmatrix} 1 \\ -2 \end{bmatrix}$, $\begin{bmatrix} 4 \\ 1 \end{bmatrix}$

(b) $\begin{bmatrix} -1 \\ -2 \end{bmatrix}$, $\begin{bmatrix} -1 \\ 1 \end{bmatrix}$, $\begin{bmatrix} 7 \\ 0 \end{bmatrix}$

(c) $\begin{bmatrix} 5 \\ -1 \end{bmatrix}$

E6 $\begin{bmatrix} 6 \\ 5 \end{bmatrix}$

E7 $a = 5$, $b = 3$

E8 (a) (i), (ii)

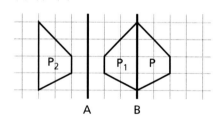

(b) (i), (ii)

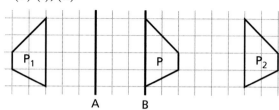

(c) Yes, the order does matter.

E9 (a) (i), (ii)

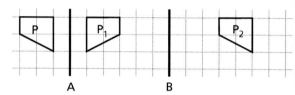

(iii) A translation of $\begin{bmatrix} 12 \\ 0 \end{bmatrix}$

(b) You can always use a translation of $\begin{bmatrix} 12 \\ 0 \end{bmatrix}$ to map P onto P_2.

E10 (a), (b) (i), (ii)

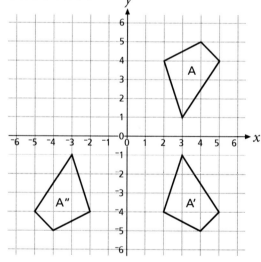

(c)

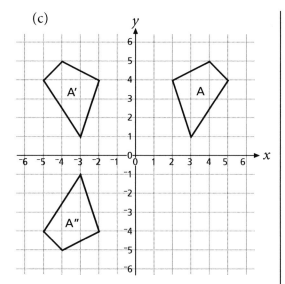

(d) No, the order does not matter.

(e) Rotation of 180° about (0, 0)

E11 (a), (b), (c)

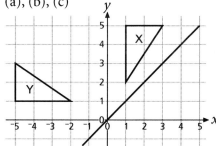

(d) Rotation of 90° anticlockwise about (0, 0)

E12 (a) (i) D

(ii) The pupil's own shape

(b) Reflection in the x-axis

E13 (a) (i) F

(ii) The pupil's own shape

(b) Reflection in the y-axis

E14 (a) (i) H

(ii) The pupil's own shape

(b) Reflection in the line $y = x$

E15 The pupil's pairs of transformations

What progress have you made? (p 166)

1 $\begin{bmatrix}6\\3\end{bmatrix}$, $\begin{bmatrix}-1\\2\end{bmatrix}$

2 (a) C   (b) E

3 (a) Reflection in the line M_2

(b) Rotation of 180° about the point P_2

(c) Rotation of 90° clockwise about the point P_3

4 (a) D   (b) G

5 The pupil's pair of transformations such as reflection in M_2 followed by a rotation of 180° about P_2

Practice booklet

Sections A to D (p 63)

1 (a) $\begin{bmatrix}3\\-6\end{bmatrix}$, $\begin{bmatrix}6\\2\end{bmatrix}$, $\begin{bmatrix}4\\-8\end{bmatrix}$

(b) Two column vectors that add to give $\begin{bmatrix}10\\-3\end{bmatrix}$ (and keep the boat on the lake!)

2 (a) Isosceles triangle

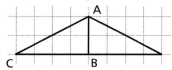

(b) Parallelogram

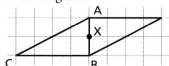

3 (a) L   (b) L   (c) D

(d) E   (e) G   (f) D

4 (a) A translation of $\begin{bmatrix} 2 \\ -4 \end{bmatrix}$

(b) A reflection in the line L_1

(c) A rotation of 180° about the point Z

(d) A rotation of 90° clockwise about the point Y

(e) A rotation of 180° about the point X

(f) A reflection in the line L_4

(g) A translation of $\begin{bmatrix} 0 \\ -6 \end{bmatrix}$

(h) A rotation of 90° clockwise about the point X

(i) A rotation of 90° anticlockwise about the point X

(j) A rotation of 90° clockwise about the point X

5 (a), (b)

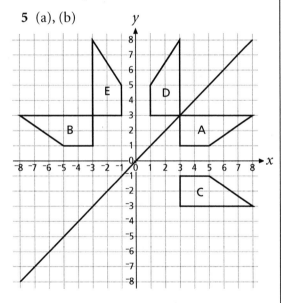

(c) (i) Reflection in the y-axis

(ii) Rotation of 180° about $(0, 0)$

(iii) Rotation of 90° clockwise about $(0, 0)$

Section E (p 66)

1 $\begin{bmatrix} 11 \\ 1 \end{bmatrix}$

2 $a = {}^-5, b = 2$

3 (a) (i)

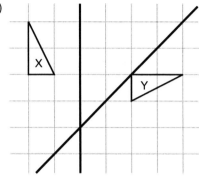

(ii) Rotation of 90° clockwise about the point of intersection of lines A and B

(b) The pupil's own shapes and images. The two reflections always give the same image as a rotation of 90° clockwise about the point of intersection of lines A and B.

4 (a) G   (b) H

5 (a) 'Rotate 180° about the point P_1' and then 'Translate by $\begin{bmatrix} 1 \\ -4 \end{bmatrix}$'

(b) 'Translate by $\begin{bmatrix} 1 \\ -4 \end{bmatrix}$' and then

'Reflect in line L'

(c) 'Rotate 90° anticlockwise about the point P_2' and then 'Reflect in line L'

(d) 'Rotate 180° about the point P_1' and then 'Translate by $\begin{bmatrix} 1 \\ -4 \end{bmatrix}$'

㉓ Trial and improvement

Essential

Spreadsheet program

Practice booklet pages 68 and 69

Ⓐ Introducing the method (p 167)

◊ Students can try these problems for themselves and their methods can be discussed. They should find that problem 1 can be solved directly by working backwards from the answer but that problem 2 cannot. However, it can be solved by trial and improvement. Problems 3 and 4 can be contrasted in a similar way. Of course, problems 2 and 4 can be solved by direct algebraic methods but it not intended that pupils consider these at this stage. All the problems have whole number answers.

There is no need for pupils to record their trials in a systematic way at this stage. The whole section could be done orally.

Ⓑ Being systematic (p 168)

The problems in this section have whole number or exact decimal solutions.

◊ Pupils can finish off problem 2, recording their trials in a table like the one on the page. They should record their trials clearly for each question, in a table or otherwise.

◊ Pupils can play a game in threes as follows.
  • One player thinks of two numbers (which can be decimals).

- The player then works out the product of the two numbers and the difference between the two numbers and tells the other two players these results.
- The other two players try to find the numbers and the winner is the one who finds them first.

ℂ **Not exactly** (p 170)

Pupils find the non-exact decimal solutions correct to 1 d.p.

◊ You will need to discuss the issue of accuracy carefully. The aim of the approach on page 170 (to finding a solution to 1 decimal place) is to 'sandwich' the solution between two adjacent decimals with 2 decimal places. We then know the digit in the second decimal place and the solution can be found correct to 1 d.p.

Of course we only actually need to look at the area for width 3.65 cm (24.2725 cm^2 – too big) to see that the width must lie between 3.6 and 3.65 and therefore must be 3.6, correct to 1 decimal place. However, it is the issue of accuracy that pupils often find most tricky and many will find the 'sandwiching' approach easier to understand at this stage.

Some pupils may decide that 3.6 must be the result correct to 1 d.p. as the area for 3.6 cm (23.76 cm^2) is nearer to the required area of 24 cm^2 than the area for 3.7 cm (24.79 cm^2). Although this approach will work for many problems, it does not always produce the correct result and should be discouraged.

C3 This has more than one solution although it is intended that pupils look for the positive solution.

C4 Pupils should find that n lies between 1.9 and 1.91. Some pupils may not see immediately that the second decimal place must be a 0.

𝔻 **Using a spreadsheet** (p 172)

Spreadsheet program

This section introduces pupils to using a spreadsheet to solve trial and improvement problems. Again, the approach of 'sandwiching' the solution between two adjacent decimals is used.

◊ After finding that there is a solution between 8 (in row 10) and 9 (in row 11), some teachers have found it useful to insert nine rows between rows 8 and 9. These rows can then have the numbers 8.1, 8.2, 8.3 and so on placed in column A, and corresponding values in columns C and E. This can strongly reinforce the concept behind the search method.

D5 This has more than one solution although it is unlikely that pupils will look for the negative one.

Ⓐ **Introducing the method** (p 167)

A1 28

A2 39

A3 48 and 49

A4 41, 42 and 43

A5 (a) 8 cm wide and 24 cm long

(b) 21 cm wide and 63 cm long

A6 19 cm wide and 22 cm long

A7 $n = 121$

A8 $n = 16$

A9 $n = 28$

Ⓑ **Being systematic** (p 168)

B1 49 and 52

B2 $n = 69$

B3 $n = 5.7$

B4 6.2 and 13.2

B5 9.5 cm wide and 11 cm long

B6 3.6 cm wide and 10.8 cm long

Ⓒ **Not exactly** (p 170)

C1 8.2 cm (to 1 d.p.)

C2 4.5 cm (to 1 d.p.)

C3 2.7 (or ⁻3.7) (to 1 d.p.)

C4 1.9 (to 1 d.p.)

C5 3.3 (to 1 d.p.)

C6 Length 10.6 cm, width 5.3 cm, height 2.7 cm (to 1 d.p.)

Ⓓ **Using a spreadsheet** (p 172)

D1 9.67 cm (to 2 d.p.)

D2 6.83 cm (to 2 d.p.)

D3 5.31 (to 2 d.p.)

D4 16.83 (to 2 d.p.)

D5 12.76 (or ⁻11.76) (to 2 d.p.)

D6 7.937 (to 3 d.p.)

D7 1.847 (to 3 d.p.)

What progress have you made? (p 173)

1 32, 33 and 34

2 Width is 4.5 cm and length is 5.5 cm (to 1 d.p.)

3 6.8 (or ⁻5.8) (to 1 d.p.)

Practice booklet

Sections A and B (p 68)

1 46 and 47

2 42, 43 and 44

3 19 cm wide and 26 cm long

4 $n = 78$

5 29 and 33

6 $n = 2.1$

7 $n = 2.6$

8 Width is 3.6 cm and length is 18 cm

Section C (p 69)

1 Width is 4.7 cm and length is 7.7 cm (to 1 d.p.)

2 4.5 cm (to 1 d.p.)

3 $n = 3.3$ (to 1 d.p.)

4 $x = 4.4$ (to 1 d.p.)

5 $x = 5.8$ (to 1 d.p.)

6 Width 26.4 cm, height 36.4 cm, length 72.8 cm (to 1 d.p.)

Spot the errors (p 174)

Pupils have to find common mistakes and correct them. Most of the mistakes are based on actual pupils' work.

> *'Good advice – I made the mistake of them doing it all and then going through it … I would have been better doing say 10 a lesson.'*

> *'With revision for SATs this was **excellent**. The students enjoyed the format and found it valuable as a revision stimulus.'*

◊ One way to organise this work is for the pupils to first work individually on a small number of questions. (They may be less likely to forget what the questions are about if they work on only a small number at one time.) Then they can compare their results in pairs or small groups, discussing where they think the pupils have gone wrong. The teacher can go through the questions, drawing together the pupils' ideas.

Encourage all pupils to try to explain orally, or in writing, why they think each mistake was made.

◊ Each answer includes a description of where the pupil has probably gone wrong.

1 There are three pieces and one of them is shaded so the pupil has written $\frac{1}{3}$.
But the pieces are not equal.
The fraction that is shaded is $\frac{1}{4}$.

2 You cannot have 2.5 minibuses as you can't have half a minibus. The pupil has not correctly interpreted the result.
You would need 3 minibuses.

3 The pupil has written three thousand (3000) and then 48 to produce 300 048.
But now the 3 is not in the thousands column.
The correct answer is 3048.

4 The pupil seems to be treating any number after the point as centimetres.
But 4.7 metres is equivalent to 4 metres and 70 centimetres.
The correct answer is 4.07 metres

5 The pupil has found the perimeter of the rectangle instead of the area.
The area is $4 \times 3 = 12\,\text{cm}^2$.

6 The division is the wrong way round.
The correct answer is $5 \div 10 = 0.5$ so each packet cost £0.50 or 50p.

7 The pupil has added the 3 to the tenths column instead of the units column.
The correct answer is 15.6

8 The pupil thinks there are only 100 metres in a kilometre instead of 1000.
The correct answer is $2000 \div 1000 = 2\,\text{km}$.

9 The pupil thinks there are only 100 grams in a kilogram instead of 1000.
The correct answer is $1000 - 20 = 980\,\text{g}$.

10 9 is not prime as 3 is a factor of 9.
The correct list is 3, 5, 7, 11, and 13.

11 The subtraction is the wrong way round.
The correct answer is 12.

12 The pupil has divided by the percentage. The first part has the right answer as 10% happens to be equivalent to $\frac{1}{10}$. But 5% is not equivalent to $\frac{1}{5}$ so you do not divide by 5 to find 5%.
The correct answer to (b) is £2.

13 The calculation is correct but the result has not been correctly written as an amount of money.

The bars cost £5.20.

14 The 74 has not been correctly lined up.

The correct answer is 1073.

15 8 ÷ 4 has been calculated first instead of 20 + 8, possibly on a scientific calculator without keying in brackets.

The correct answer is (20 + 8) ÷ 4 = 7.

16 The calculation has been worked from left to right. But multiplication takes priority over subtraction.

The correct answer is 4.

17 3:00 has been treated as 300 and, as 300 − 50 = 250, the time has been given as 2:50.

The correct time is 2:10.

18 The pupil has ordered according to the values of the digits, ignoring place value.

The correct order is:
0.004, 0.0065, 0.03, 0.2, 0.5

19 Remove the decimal point and 129 is the largest number. The pupil has misinterpreted the value of the digits after the decimal point.

The largest number is 0.23.

20 Although each diagonal line bisects the rectangle, neither is a line of symmetry.

Only the horizontal and vertical lines are lines of symmetry.

21 The highest **frequency** is 9 but this is not the mode.

The mode is the colour blue as it is the colour with the highest frequency.

22 The pupil has treated these events as equally likely. It is true that it will be wet or dry tomorrow but in general these events are not equally likely. You may be able to state a sensible probability that it will be wet tomorrow in a particular area but you will base this on, say, knowledge of weather patterns.

So, in the absence of other information, you cannot decide on the probability that it will be wet tomorrow.

23 The pupil has multiplied all given lengths instead of splitting the shape into rectangles.

The correct area is 21 cm².

24 The outer scale on the protractor has been read to give 60°.

The inner scale gives the correct answer of 120°.

25 Although each diagonal line bisects the parallelogram, neither is a line of symmetry here.

A parallelogram has no lines of symmetry in general. The only parallelograms with lines of symmetry are the special cases: rhombuses or rectangles (including squares).

26 There are three colours and one of them is red so the pupil has written $\frac{1}{3}$. The three colours on the spinner are not equally likely so the probability is not $\frac{1}{3}$.

The correct probability is $\frac{1}{4}$.

27 The pupil has multiplied all given lengths.

The volume is 2 × 4 × 5 = 40 cm³.

28 The pupil has multiplied all given lengths before dividing by 2.

The correct area is (3 × 4) ÷ 2 = 6 cm².

29 The pupil has gone the wrong way from a multiple of 10, in this case reading from 50 to obtain 54°.

The correct answer is 46°.

 **Stretchers**

Ⓐ Darts (p 178)

This set of problems can lead to further investigation.

◊ After A1 to A3, pupils could restrict themselves to two darts and three sectors and investigate the numbers of different totals for different types of board. Questions might arise such as:

- How many different totals are there when all three numbers are the same?
- How many different totals are there when two numbers are the same?
- Is it possible to design a board that gives only two totals?
- What is the maximum number of different totals?
- How do you design a dartboard that gives six different totals?

◊ After A4 and A5, pupils could consider four-sector dartboards. They could try to design boards that give the most and least different totals (and see if all the different numbers of totals in between can be achieved).

Then the more general question can be posed: 'Can you find a rule for the maximum number of different totals with two darts on a dartboard with n sectors?'

Ⓑ Minimal measuring (p 179)

B3 Pupils are likely to find this question very difficult. Some will see that a set of strips 1 cm, 3 cm and 9 cm can be used to make every length up to 13 cm but will find it difficult to see that the fourth strip can be 27 cm. They could appeal to the trebling pattern in 1, 3, 9, … to make the hypothesis that 27 cm is the next strip and then set themselves the challenge of finding how to make all lengths up to 40 cm with these strips.

Ⓐ Darts (p 178)

A1 (a) (i) 5 (ii) 14 (b) 4, 5, 6, 9, 10, 14

A2 (a) 2, 3, 4, 5, 6, 8 (b) 4, 5, 6, 7, 8
(c) 2, 3, 4, 5, 6 (d) 2, 7, 12

A3 (a) 5, 8, 11 (b) 2, 3, 5
(c) 2, 2, 9 or 2, 9, 9

A4 2, 5, 8, 11, 14, 17, 20

A5 (a) There are many possible solutions such as 1, 1, 1, 2 or 2, 2, 2, 1

(b) There are many possible solutions, for example: 1, 2, 5, 7 or 5, 6, 8, 12

Ⓑ Minimal measuring (p 179)

All numbers are lengths in centimetres.

B1 (a) 10, 3 (b) 4, 6, 8, 11, 13, 15
(c) (i) 9, 14, 16, 18 (ii) 19
(d) 2, 7, 12, 17, 20
(e) 1, 2, 4, 8, 16 The longest is 31 cm.

B2 1, 2, 3, 4, 5, 6, 7, 8, 9, 11, 12, 13, 14, 17

B3 1, 3, 9, 27 The longest length is 40 cm.

Review 4 (p 180)

1

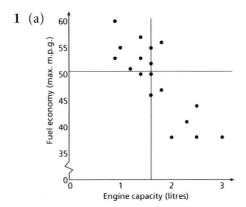

(scatter graph: x-axis "Score in test 1" from 0 to 20, y-axis "Score in test 2" from 0 to 20)

There is positive correlation between the two scores.

2 (a) $n = 5$ (b) $x = 7$

3 58

4 (a) 128°   (b) 140°   (c) 36°
   (d) 82°   (e) 84°

5 0.64

6 (a) $a = 53°, b = 127°, c = 127°$
   (b) b and c

7 (a) E   (b) D

8 (a) A reflection in the line M_2
   (b) A translation of $\begin{bmatrix} 8 \\ -8 \end{bmatrix}$
   (c) A rotation of 180° about R

9 (a) A reflection in the line M_1
   (b) A rotation of 180° about P
   (c) A rotation of 90° anticlockwise about R
   (b) A translation of $\begin{bmatrix} -8 \\ -8 \end{bmatrix}$

10 (a) E
   (b) A rotation of 180° about P

11 (a) H
   (b) A reflection in the line M_1

12 (a) 55°   (b) 102°   (c) 120°

13 (a) $5n + 2$ (b) $3n + 44$
   (c) $5n + 2 = 3n + 44$ with solution
      $n = 21$ so there are 21 sweets in a bag

14 Trials leading to $x = 5.8$ (to 1 d.p.)
   (or $x = {}^-6.8$)

15 (a) $f = 9$ (b) $g = 12$ (c) $x = 12$
   (d) $h = 1.5$ (e) $y = 5$ (f) $k = 2$

16 99°

Mixed questions 4 (Practice booklet p 70)

1 (a)

(scatter graph: x-axis "Engine capacity (litres)" from 0 to 3, y-axis "Fuel economy (max. m.p.g.)" from 0 to 60)

   (b) Larger engines tend to do fewer miles to the gallon
   (c) There is negative correlation.

2 (a) 29°   (b) 63°   (c) 290°

3 (a) $x = 2.5$ (b) $p = 5$
   (c) $m = 4$ (d) $n = 7$

4 (a) Rotational symmetry of order 8
   (b) 32
   (c) One pair of parallel lines from:
      AF and BE, AD and HE
      BG and CF, CH and DG
   (d) (i) u and v (ii) y and z
      (iii) x and w

5 (a) $f = 2$ (b) $t = 5$
   (c) $n = 6$ (d) $y = 7$

6 (a), (b), (c), (e)

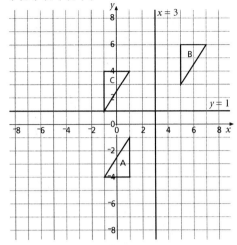

(d) Rotation through 180° about the point (3, 1)

(f) Rotation of 180° about (0, 0)

7 (a) $3x - 30 = 180$ with the pupil's explanation

(b) $x = 70$

(c) 40°

8 (a) 130°
Angle BCD = 130° (angles at a point)
Angle ADE = Angle BCD
        (corresponding angles)
        = 130°

(b) 80°
Angle PRQ = 55° (angles on a
                straight line)
Angle PQR = 45° (alternate angles)
Angle QPR = 80° (angles in a triangle

9 (a) $40 - 2n = 3n$ gives $n = 8$

(b) $50 - 4n = n$ gives $n = 10$

10 1.4 cm